Political Development

and Social Change

in Ghana:

GHANA UNDER NKRUMAH

A Study of the Influence of Kwame Nkrumah
and the Role of Ideas in Rapid Social Change

Political Development

and Social Change

in Ghana:

GHANA UNDER NKRUMAH

A Study of the Influence of Kwame Nkrumah
and the Role of Ideas in Rapid Social Change

By

FRANCIS A. BOTCHWAY

BLACK ACADEMY PRESS, INC.

BUFFALO, NEW YORK USA

Published by

BLACK ACADEMY PRESS, INC.

135 University Avenue

Buffalo, New York 14214

* * * * * *

Box 104, Owerri, Nigeria

* * * * * *

41 Leigham Vale, London, S.W. 16

ISBN 0-87831-068-1

Library of Congress Catalog Card Number: 74-177290

Copyright 1972 by Francis A. Botchway

Printed in the United States of America

TABLE OF CONTENTS

TABLE OF CONTENTS   (Continued)

THIS book deals with the impact of Kwame
Nkrumah and the Convention People's Party on
social change and political development in Ghana.
The purpose of this book is to analyse the nature
of the impact of Kwame Nkrumah and the Convention
People's Party and the role of ideas in rapid
social change and political development in Ghana,
with the view to understanding the reasons
underlying the kind of responses that have
manifested themselves on the part of the
traditional elites in their encounter with Nkrumah
and the C.P.P. The period covered in this book is
approximately from 1949 to 1965.

In writing this book I have confined myself
to an analysis of the ideas of Nkrumah and the
role of the C.P.P. The historical perspective is
provided as a prelude to the emergence of Nkrumah
and the C.P.P. I have tried to reconstruct the
history of the emergence of nationalism in Ghana
in terms of the light it would shed on the C.P.P.
and the consequent fall of Nkrumah. However,
there are two points in the standard historical
interpretation with which I find myself unable to
agree. Bob Fitch and Mary Oppenheimer ("Ghana:
End of an Illusion", •Monthly Review, XVIII,•3
July-August, 1966) argue that the C.P.P. rose as a
champion of petty bourgeois interests and that
Nkrumah's fall was due to his failure to pursue
adequately Marxist policies, in essence, that
Nkrumah was not radical enough. This is rather a
simplistic view. Henry Bretton •(The Rise and
Fall of Kwame Nkrumah,• New York, 1966), on the
other hand, argues that Nkrumah was too radical.
My own view is that Nkrumah's failure was due to
his transformation of the C.P.P., an emotionally
aroused mass independence movement, into a
bourgeois dictatorship, and to his inability to
resolve the conflict between the C.P.P. activists
and the other nationalist elites within the
country.

Throughout this book I have refrained from
describing Nkrumah as a charismatic leader,
because to do so, would be "to confuse temporary
popularity with something more· profound, thus
changing a momentary attribute into a 'credential'
Nkrumah could use to sustain personal power"
(David Apter, "Nkrumah, Charisma, and the Coup",

8

Daedalus , Summer 1968, pp.757-792). But in the perspective of history, I hold to my view of him as an exceptional leader in an exceptional stage of Ghanaian history, and as the one who more than any other Ghanaian leader politicized the Ghanaian people. Future generations will judge him in the context of his times.

Chapter One of this book deals with the historical background of the evolution of protest movements and the emergence of nationalism in Ghana; Chapter Two deals with the evolution of the Convention People's Party as the first political party in Ghana that politicized the Ghanaian people *en masse* ; Chapter Three deals with Nkrumaism as a national ideology, and Chapter Four deals with Marimization of political power, i.e., the acquisition of the highest possible degree of political power, and a theoretical discussion of the various approaches used by Nkrumah in maximization of his political power and that of the C.P.P. The characteristics of a given stage in the process are distinctive, in that they are unique to that stage. I have also indicated the analytical relations to preceding stages in the process of maximizing political power which make the succeeding stages possible, and have indicated the universe for which the generality of common and distinctive variables is probable. Chapter Five deals with the role of the C.P.P. as an agent of social change. Chapter Six deals with the role of education in the process of social change and is an analysis of the program of the C.P.P., and Chapter Seven deals with Nkrumah's stated principles and program for industrialization and the development of a Socialist Society in Ghana.

To some critics of Nkrumah and the C.P.P., a demand for objectivity is an impossible plea; to his admirers a plea for objectivity is like asking a religious fanatic to take a non-partisan attitude toward his religion. And the consequence is a chorus of denunciation and praise so contradictory as to suggest that scholarly objectivity is an impossible task.

I must observe in passing, though that when convulsions, such as social and political revolutions, occur, judgment on the deposed leadership is sometimes passed by the firing squad and sometimes by sheer public outrage. But, I am afraid, never in history has there been a leader

so evil that he has not been successful in
subsequent generations in finding a defender.

Some of the observations presented in this
book are doubtless common knowledge--although they
are by no means commonly acknowledged. At times
even the most simple and familiar phenomena take
on a new aspect when seen, not in isolation but in
the context of a broader stream of events. My
main emphasis has been on the correlations between
events and processes which at first glance may
seem far apart and unrelated. These events and
processes have, as far as I know, scarcely been
studied methodically. Yet they are, so it seems
to me, the basic and the most serious events of
the modernization process in Africa.

In the pages that follow, my indebtedness to
many writers and scholars on whose research and
interpretation I have drawn will be obvious. I
feel called upon to acknowledge here, however, the
special debt I owe to Professor Dennis Austin,
whose painstaking reconstruction of the
decolonization process in Ghana, published as
•Politics in Ghana•,was indispensable in designing
my book.

This book attempts to construct from the
assemblage of events and processes a coherent
picture of the attempted transformation of
Ghanaian society and to convey an awareness of the
grave perils with which it was fraught under the
Nkrumah regime.

It is impossible for me to give recognition
to everyone who has helped in molding my
intellectual outlook. Of those mentors to whom I
am greatly indebted, I would like to mention the
following: Henry A. Botchway, who first introduced
me to scholarship; Professors L. Gray Cowan and
Wayne Wilcox who helped me so much when I was an
undergraduate at Columbia University; Professors
William T.R. Fox, Oliver J. Lissitzyn, both of
Columbia University, and the late Dr. W. Jordan of
the United Nations Department of Political and
Security Council Affairs, who introduced me to
world politics, international organization and
international law; Professors George Ginsburgs and
C. Neale Ronning of the Graduate Faculty of the
New School for Social Research, and Mr. Ralph
Townley of the United Nations Development Program,
who enhanced my knowledge and understanding of
international law and international political

10

institutions; Professor Saul K. Padover who, in
the graduate seminars at the New School for Social
Research, introduced me to the 'genius' of
American political thought and institutions;
Professors Norman Birnbaum and Dennis H. Wrong,
who introduced me to political sociology and
problems in sociological theory; and Professor
Adamantia Pollis who, in her graduate seminar on
Comparative Political Methodology, introduced me
to comparative institutions and empirical
political science and also to developmental
economics. My thanks are due to many of my
colleagues in the Department of Political Science
and Sociology of the Graduate Faculty of the New
School for Social Research. But, perhaps, most of
all I am grateful for the intellectual atmosphere
that prevails at the New School, an atmosphere in
which intellectual flexibility and a democratic
concept of higher education flourish.

For financial assistance I am indebted to the
National Baptist Convention, U.S.A., Inc., for a
year's fellowship; to the Institute of
International Education for a year's fellowship;
and to the Government of Ghana for six years of
financial assistance.

I am greatly indebted to Professors Adamantia
Pollis, C. Neal Ronning and Stanley Diamond for
commenting on the manuscript and making helpful
suggestions. My special thanks go to Professor
Adamantia Pollis who not only helped me in such
tasks as revising the manuscript, selecting and
pondering material of documentation, checking
references and correcting grammar, but took the
book in her comprehensive care, devoting to it the
unusual gifts of her mind.

Finally, I want to express my special thanks
to my parents, who made it possible for me to have
an education and imbued me with a sympathetic
understanding of human existence.

Any errors or omissions in this book are
entirely my own responsibility.

NEW YORK, N.Y., 1971   F.A.B.

HISTORICAL BACKGROUND : THE EVOLUTION
OF PROTEST MOVEMENTS IN GHANA

AT the Ninth International Convention of the
Student Movement at Indianapolis in 1923, Dr.
Aggrey1 postulated the hypothesis of the
inevitable evolution of a youth movement in
Africa. Commenting on the restlessness of the
colonial peoples in Africa, he said:

> There is a Youth Movement coming in
> Africa that some day may startle the world.
> This restlessness all over Africa stands for
> self-discovery, selfrealization. It tells of
> power just breaking through. The great
> continent has been asleep for a long time.
> It is now waking....This Niagara, if allowed
> to sweep through the land, may deluge and
> inundate cities and towns and bring forth
> ruin. If under God it can be harnessed, it
> will turn a dynamo and generate electricity
> that will illuminate that great continent,
> chase out the utter darkness and bring a new
> Africa into being....There is a new Africa
> coming today, and it is a challenge to
> civilization.2

In his autobiography, Nkrumah tells of his
admiration for Dr. Aggrey, whom he had hoped
would become his intellectual mentor. He
writes:
> To me he seemed the most remarkable man
> that I had ever met and I had the deepest
> affection for him. He possessed intense
> vitality and enthusiasm and a most infectious
> laugh that seemed to bubble up from his
> heart, and he was a very great orator. It
> was through him that my nationalism was first
> aroused....It was because of my great
> admiration for Aggrey, both as man and as
> scholar, that I first formed the idea of
> furthering my studies in the United

But Dr. Aggrey died before Nkrumah came to the
United States to further his studies. And just as
Dr. Aggrey had lived and worked for Africa and
became known as the Aggrey of Africa, so was
Nkrumah to become known not just as Nkrumah of
Ghana, but as Nkrumah of Africa.

It would be misleading to think that the return of Nkrumah to Ghana marked the beginning of nationalism in Ghana. The rise of nationalism had long been in gestation before Nkrumah left for the United States in 1934. But it must be pointed out that Nkrumah brought a new perspective to the struggle for political emancipation.

Though this is not a study in political historiography, it seems logical to give a brief account of the rise of nationalism in Ghana in order to provide the basis for an understanding of the evolution of the Convention People's Party and the subsequent use of the Convention People's Party by Nkrumah as a vehicle for the construction of socialism in Ghana.

THE COMING OF EUROPEANS

There has been a longstanding antipathy to Europeans and colonialism in Ghana. This antipathy was one of the forces behind the emergence of nationalism as well as a force which the nationalist movements can harness.*4 The origins of this antipathy, lay, in part at least, in the mistreatment of Ghanaians by the European colonizers. On January 19, 1482, the first official contact with Europe was made with Portuguese navigators in search of gold, ivory and spices.*5 On January 20, 1482, Diego da Azambuja, the leader of the Portuguese expeditionary force summoned Nana Kwamena Ansa, Chief of Elmina, to the beach and made known to him the reasons of the expedition, and a request from King John II, son of King Alfonso, to build a fort at Elmina beach. In denying this request, Nana Kwabena Ansa made an extemporaneous speech which is worth quoting in full because of the richness of the Akan language and the natural eloquence of the speaker. It is also an index to the intellectual development and sophistication of a people:

> I am not insensible to the high honour which your great master the Chief of Portugal has this day conferred upon me. His friendship I have always endeavoured to merit by the strictness of my dealing with the Portuguese, and by my constant exertions to procure an immediate lading for the vessels. But never until this day did I observe such a difference in the appearance of his subjects; they have hitherto been meanly attired; were easily contented with the commodities they received; and so far from wishing to continue

in this country, were never happy until they
could complete their lading and return.   Now
I remark a strange difference.   A great
number of richly dressed men are anxious to
be allowed to build houses, and to continue
among us. Men of such eminence, conducted by
a commander who from his own account seems to
have descended from the God who made day and
night, can never bring themselves to endure
the hardships of this climate; nor would they
here be able to procure any of the luxuries
that abound in their own country.   The
passions that are common to us all men will
therefore inevitably bring on disputes; and
it is far preferable that both our nations
should continue on the same footing as they
have hitherto done, allowing your ships to
come and go as usual; the desire of seeing
each other occasionally will preserve peace
between us.   The sea and the land being
always neighbors are continually at variance
attempting to subdue the land, and the land
with equal obstinacy resolving to oppose the
sea.•6

When the request was turned down, Diego da
Azambuja, with his expeditionary forces, fortified
the beach by force of arms and went ahead and
built Elmina Castle.   Thus began the process of
colonization.   The Dutch, disregarding the Papal
Bull of 1493, which gave the Portuguese the
monopoly of trade in West Africa, followed

next at around 1593.   Then came the Swedes in
1640, the Danes, the English, and the
Brandenburgers in 1638.   These were followed by
missionary societies, who by mid-nineteenth
century had penetrated inland, built missionary
schools and colleges, and then embarked on
converting the people.   The governments of these
missionary societies, however, . remained
indifferent to the efforts of their Christian
brethren.   They were mainly interested in trade
not religion.

What, therefore, were the activities of these
early European visitors to the Gulf of Guinea?
They were mainly interested in trade, especially
in gold, thus the "Gold Coast".   But the trade in
gold was not all.   The initial practice of
exchanging commodities for gold was short-lived.
Their interest shifted from material goods to
human traffic, i.e., slavery.   And the first few

Africans that were sent to Europe went there for
domestic service. Some of these Africans were
presented to the Papacy as gifts by the
Portuguese. The Pope, in turn, rewarded these
early adventurers with the celebrated Papal Bull.
Nothing much happened in the Gold Coast until the
discovery of the New World, and the West Indian
islands. This discovery intensified the traffic
in human beings. The French, the Dutch, the
Danes, and the English, all took part in this
inhuman venture, the brutality and ferocity of
which

has been recorded by none other than a Portuguese
eyewitness, E.B. D'Auvergne, in his book Human
Livestock•. We quote his entire description for
it presents graphically the nature of this inhuman
institution:

> On the 8th day of August 1444, very
> early in the morning on account of the heat,
> the mariners began to assemble their lighters
> and to disembark their captives, according to
> their orders. Which captives were gathered
> in a field, and marvellous it was to see
> among them some of a rosy whiteness, fair and
> well-made; others less white verging on grey;
> others again as black as moles, as various in
> their complexions as in their shapes....and
> what heart was so hard as not to be moved to
> pity by the sight of this multitude, some
> with bowed heads and tearful countenances,
> others groaning dolorously and with eyes
> uplifted towards heaven, as if to implore
> help from the Father of all mankind; while
> there were others who covered their faces
> with their hands and flung themselves down
> upon the ground, and some again who gave vent
> to their sorrow in a dirge, after the manner
> of their country; and although we could not
> understand the words well we appreciated the
> depth of their distress. And now to
> aggravate their woe, men came to parcel them
> out into five distinct lots, to do which they
> tore the son from his father, the wife from
> her husband, the brother from his brethren.
> No tie of blood or comradeship was respected;
> each was thrown into a place by chance. O
> irresistible fortune, thou which ridest
> roughest over the affairs of the world, bring
> to the knowledge of these most unhappy folk
> those ultimate truths from which they may
> receive consolation! And yet that are

charged with this division into lots, deplore
so great a misery, and observe how these
unhappy ones embrace one another so tightly
that it needs no little strength to tear them
apart. Such a division indeed, was not to be
effected without great trouble, since parents
and children finding themselves in different
groups, would run back to each other -
mothers clutched up their children and ran
away with them, caring not about the blows
they received so long as their little ones
should not be torn from them. After this
toilsome fashion was the task of division
accomplished, the work being rendered more
difficult by crowds which flocked from the
neighbouring towns and villages, neglecting
their work to see the novel sight. And some
of these spectators moved to tears, others
chattering, they made a tumult which hindered
those charged with the business. The Infante
(Don Henry) mounted on a powerful horse,
destined to take his own share, some 46
souls, but threw it back into the common
stock, taking pleasure only in the thought of
so many souls being redeemed from perdition.
And truly, his hope was not vain, since so
soon as they learned the language, with very
little trouble, these people became
Christians; and I who write this history saw
afterwards in the town of Lagos (in Portugal)
young men and women, the offspring of these,
born in the country, as good and genuine
Christians as if they had been descended from
the generations first baptised under the
dispensation of Christ.

In 1872 the Danish and Dutch governments
withdrew from the country, while the Colonial
Office in Britain decided to turn the country into
a crown colony. Consequently, the coastal region
of the country became a British Crown Colony. The
northern part of the country became a British
Protectorate in 1898, and Ashanti was annexed in
1901. In 1919, at the end of World War 1, when
Germany was defeated and deprived of all of her
colonial possessions, part of the German
Protectorate of Togoland became a British Mandated
Territory. At the end of World War 11, Togoland
became a Trust Territory under Britain. Thus, the
process of colonization was completed in 1919 when
the country officially became known as the British
Colony of the Gold Coast.7

This process of colonization was, however, not a peaceful process. The very nature of the process itself subsequently produced the conditions that gave rise to the emergence of protest movements in the Gold Coast. What, therefore, was the nature of the process?

In 1865 a Select Committee of the British Parliament reported in a study that "all further extensions of territory (in West Africa), or assumption of government or new treaties offering any protection to native tribes would be inexpedient; and that the object of our policy would be to encourage in the natives the exercise of those qualities, which may render it possible for us more and more to transfer to them the administration of all the Government, with a view to an ultimate withdrawal from all except probably Sierra Leone." This declaration of Parliament was subsequently discarded and replaced by the Foreign Jurisdiction Act of 1843, an Act which legalized the exercise of British jurisdiction and authority beyond the limits of British territory on the coast whenever by treaty or by usage such jurisdiction and authority had already been secured or might conceivably be secured in the future.

Prior to the Foreign Jurisdiction Act of 1843, a tripartite peace treaty had been signed between the Ashanti, British, and the coastal allies, comprising the Adas, Akims, Akwomos, Denkyeras, Ga-Adangbes, Gas (old allies of Ashantis), Fantes, and the Krobos. This treaty, which was to create the Gold Coast Protectorate, was signed with one Captain George Maclean at the Cape Coast Castle.

With the coming into force of the Foreign Jurisdiction Act of 1843, Captain George Maclean was appointed the first colonial judge in the Gold Coast. He subsequently became Governor of the Gold Coast. A year after the Act of 1843, the Fanti States appended their signatures through their traditional rulers to a treaty commonly known as the Bond of 1844.

The Bond of 1844 recognized British jurisdiction over cases involving murder, robbery and other serious crimes. It also accorded Britain trading rights. In essence, it was a treaty which gave •de jure• recognition to the relationship that had developed between the

British traders and administrators and the Coastal
peoples.

The Bond of 1844 was followed by treaties of
"friendship and protection" between the British
and the other nonFanti chiefs along the coast.
Britain subsequently was to enter into alliance
with the chiefs of the coastal areas against the
Ashantis.

The Ashanti Kingdom was a powerful military
confederation composed of the Akan-speaking people
in the center of the Gold Coast. This military
confederation had become possible as a result of
the initiative of King Osei Tutu, who reigned from
1700-1730. He was also to effect this unity of
the Akans with the aid of his spiritual advisor,
Okonfo Anokye, who created the myth of the Golden
Stool as a symbol of unity by declaring that in
the Golden Stool was embedded the spirit and soul
of the Ashanti nation.

Tradition has it that Okonfo Anckye summoned
all the Akan chiefs to Kumasi (capital of Ashanti)
on one Friday, and that he drew down from Heaven a
black cloud from which issued the rumblings of
thunder and a stool. The stool is said to have
descended from Heaven and rested upon the knees of
King Osei Tutu. A collection of hairs and
fingernails were extracted from the chiefs and the
queen-mothers of the various Akan states and used
in preparing a black potion. This potion was
mixed with native wine and drunk by all the chiefs
and queen-mothers who swore allegiance to King
Osei Tutu and to the Ashanti nation.

Tradition again has it that Okonfo Anokye
proclaimed that the stool is an embodiment of the
soul of the Ashanti people and that the stool is
the fountain of their honor, greatness and
welfare. The stool was never to fall into the
hands of an enemy. Should it fall into captivity,
the Ashanti nation would disintegrate. Only on
rare occasions was it to be brought out for
ceremonial purposes, and the ground on which it
was placed must be covered with an elephant skin.

In 1873, the Ashantis declared war on the
coastal peoples, but with the help of the British
the Ashantis were defeated. The King of Ashanti
was reduced to the King of Kumasi, and the various
states that had formed the Federation were granted
their independence. The Ashanti King was required

by the British to pay an indemnity of 50,000
ounces of gold to the colonial administration
every year.

In 1896 the British Government, having
decided earlier in 1874 to assume full control
over the Gold Coast, demanded that the Ashantis
should submit to their rule and also pay the long
overdue indemnity of 50,000 ounces of gold. The
King of Ashanti was not able to pay and was
arrested together with his mother and several
members of his family. They were first
incarcerated at the Elmina Castle, but an attempt
by the Ashantis to invade the Castle led to their
eventual deportation to Sierra Leone and
subsequently to the Seychelles Islands where they
remained until 1924.

The colonial Governor then administering the
Gold Coast Colony was Sir Frederick Hodgson, and
although the Ashantis had resigned themselves to
their fate, Sir Frederick Hodgson decided that as
long as the Ashantis had the Golden Stool it was
not possible to exercise effective control over
them. Sir Frederick, with a small detachment,
went to Kumasi to demand the Golden Stool. This
demand led to the Yaa Asantewa War of 1900 which
led in turn to the total defeat of the Ashantis
and of their leaders, but, it did not result in
the capture of the Golden Stool.

The total defeat of the Ashantis enabled the
British to annex Ashanti, as a conquered
territory, to the Gold Coast Colony. Whilst the
Ashantis were being conquered, Northern Ghana,
formerly known as the Northern Territories of the
Gold Coast, was being annexed by treaties with the
various chiefs. In order to exercise effective
British jurisdiction, the first battalion of the
Gold Coast Regiment was stationed in Ashanti and
thereafter the British devoted their attention to
the establishment of law and order.

With the Orders in Council published in 1902,
and with the Protectorate of Togoland becoming a
British Trust Territory at the end of World War
II, the colonization process in the Gold Coast was
completed.

Long before the completion of the
colonization process, nationalist movements were
in gestation. In the pages that follow we shall

examine the conditions that gave rise to these
movements.

THE EMERGENCE OF PROTEST MOVEMENTS

What were the conditions that gave rise to
the emergence of protest movements? They may be
said to be questions basically related to land and
honor. Ghanaians generally associate prosperity
and social status with the ownership of land. The
very nature of this value system has been the
cause of much tribal warfare and litigation. It
was, therefore, the attempt of the colonial
government to change the nature of land ownership,
i.e., from Stool lands to Crown lands that gave
rise to the emergence of protest movements.

The first indication of an organized
challenge to colonialism was the formation of the
"Aborigines Rights and Protection Society" in 1897
as a response to the decision of the then
Governor, Sir William Maxwell, to convert the
stool lands into crown lands. To comprehend the
reasons behind the formation of the above society,
it must be pointed out that land has a mystical as
well as a secular value in Ghanaian tradition.
Land belongs to the people, and the chief is only
a temporary custodian of the land, which is
communal property belonging to the ancestors.
Professor Busia writes:

> The Earth was regarded as possessing a
> spirit or power of its own which was helpful
> if propitiated, and harmful if neglected, but
> the land was also regarded as belonging to
> the ancestors. It is from them that the
> living have inherited the right to use it.•8

Prior to the formation of the Aborigines
Rights and Protection Society, the Fantse
Confederacy had been formed in 1868 to resist the
Anglo-Dutch exchange of forts and the British
refusal to pay rents to the chiefs. The genius
behind this confederation was King Ghartey IV of
Winneba, who was elected its President and who was
vested with authority to govern the Confederacy,
with the aid of a cabinet of five officials,
representing the chiefs and the elites, to assist
the King and his council of chiefs. A
Representative Legislative Assembly was proposed
by the A.R.P.S. It was to be composed of two
representatives from each district of the

Confederacy appointed by the King. The Assembly was to be responsible to the King and the chiefs of the Confederacy and was to enact legislation compatible with the interests of the people and the country.

These are some of the highlights of the Constitution adopted by the Confederacy:

SECTION 4. To erect school houses and establish schools for the education of all children within the Confederation, and to obtain the services of efficient schoolmasters.

SECTION 5. To promote agricultural and industrial pursuits and to endeavor to introduce such new plants as may hereafter become sources of profitable commerce to the country.

SECTION 6. To develop and facilitate the exploitation of the mineral and other resources of the country.

ARTICLE 26. That main roads be made, connecting various provinces or districts with one another and with the sea coast...

ARTICLE 37. That in each province or district provincial courts be established,to be presides over by the provincial assessors.

In 1871, the Executive Members of the Confederacy•9 sent a letter to the Governor of the Gold Coast informing him of the formation of the Confederacy and its objectives. The Confederacy was considered illegal and as a dangerous organization. Some of the officers were arrested and imprisoned. When the Secretary of State for the Colonies, Lord Kimberly, was informed of the arrest and imprisonment, he instructed the Judicial Assessor's Court in the Colony to stay the proceedings if the court had not already proceeded with the case. The intervention of Lord Kimberly was too late in coming and did not help the Confederacy. The Confederacy was subsequently dissolved.

The aims considered conspiratorial by the Governor were those contained in a letter to him dated November 24th, 1871. It states in full:

Sir, we the Kings, Chiefs and others assembled at Markession beg most respectfully to forward you the enclosed copy of a Constitution framed and passed by us after mature consideration.

We have united together for the express purpose of furthering the interests of our country. In the Constitution it will be observed that we contemplate means for the social improvement of our subjects and peoples, the growth of education and industrial pursuits, and in short, every good which British philanthropy may have designed for the good of the Gold Coast, but which we think is impossible for it at present to do for the country at large.

Our sole object is to improve the conditions of our peoples, not to interfere with, but to aid our benefactors on the sea coast, and we count upon your Excellency giving us at times that assistance which may be necessary to carry out our humble efforts. We beg to forward a copy of the Constitution, and of Resolutions 1 and 2, for the information of the Right Honourable, the Secretary of State for the Colonies.•10

The dissolution of the Fanti Confederacy however, did not daunt the spirit of protest of the leaders of the time. Though the "Aborigines Rights and Protection Society" was formed with the purpose of opposing a Crown Lands Bill, it also sought a democratization of the Colonial Legislature and the introduction of a government in which the executive would be responsible and accountable not to the Governor, but to the elected representatives of the people. The Society, with the failure of the Confederacy still vivid in the minds of its leaders, did not petition the Governor of the Gold Coast, but instead, sent a delegation to England to petition the Right Honorable Joseph Chamberlain, Secretary of State for the Colonies.•11

The Aborigines Rights and Protection Society had as its objectives the following:

1. To protect the rights of the Aborigines of the Gold Coast at all times by constitutional means and methods.

2. To promote and effect unity of purpose and of action among all aborigines of the Gold Coast.

3. To inculcate upon the members the importance of continued loyalty to the British Crown, and to educate them to a proper and correct understanding of the relations which have existed for about 400 (four hundred) years between Great Britain and this country.

4. To foster in the rising generation a knowledge of their historical past, and to encourage the study of the laws, customs, and institutions of the country, to promote a sound national educational policy with particular attention to agricultural, scientific and industrial training, and generally to facilitate the spread of industry and thrift in the whole country.

5. To be the medium of communication and right understanding between the Government and the people.

6. Generally to promote the interests and advancement of the aborigines of the Gold Coast in any lawful matter whatsoever.

These movements grew out of the desire to better the conditions of the traditional rulers who had accepted the legitimacy of the colonial system. Their programs were characterized by an emphasis on progress and improvement, on the spread of literacy and technical education, on the dignity of the individual and, last, on continued loyalty to the Crown. But these were only the meaningful temporal dimensions of their experiences. As we shall see later, these experiences greatly influenced the specific contours of the development of political parties in Ghana.

THE WEST AFRICAN CONGRESS

At about the beginning of the twentieth century, the leadership of the protest movement began to exhibit new characteristics--greater ability to adjust to wider horizons (total society); greater interest in widening spheres of interest; empathy with other colonial peoples; and

a growing evaluation of their roles in West Africa
in general. In 1917 a West African Congress was
called.•12 It was the first trans-territorial
conference in Africa of British West African
intellectuals. The Congress requested the
granting of self-government "so that peoples of
African descent should participate in the
government of their own country." A number of
resolutions were adopted and incorporated into a
memorandum which was subsequently presented to the
Secretary of State for the Colonies, Lord Milner,
in October 1920 by a delegation led by Casley
Hayford. The memorandum demanded,•inter alia•,
the following:•13

  a.   An elective franchise (to elect their
own representatives).

  b.   The separation of the judiciary from the
        executive so that justice may be
        administered without fear or favor.

  c.   A West African Court of Appeal.

  d.   Trial by jury for all capital offenses.

  e.   The introduction of Municipal Government
Administration into West Africa.

  f.   The retention of the West African system
        of land tenure.

  g.   The establishment of a West African
University.

  h.   The regulation of the immigration of
        Syrians and other Non-Africans into West
        Africa.

  i.   The abolition of Racial Discrimination
in the Civil Service.

  The West African Congress failed to become a
viable political movement because it lacked the
existence of a strong mass basis, the existence of
a strong politically minded leadership and a party
program. That the Congress failed to become a
viable political movement can only be explained
sociologically in that, unlike the ideological and
wholistic type of social movement, which aims at
the transformation of society or of a polity, it
was a restricted movement composed of leading
intellectuals of West Africa who met primarily to

exchange ideas and opinions. The movement was
oriented toward the attainment of specific goals
(better conditions of life for these
intellectuals) not directly related to the
concrete goal of political independence. The
goals represented the application of general
principles of justice -- such as trial by jury for
all capital offenses, an effective franchise and
abolition of racial discrimination. The movement
lacked a strong future orientation. Unlike the
ideological and wholistic social movements, the
West African Congress did not have semi-Messianic
or charismatic elements.•14

THE GOLD COAST YOUTH CONFERENCE

With the demise of the Congress, the Gold
Coast Youth Conference was formed under the aegis
of Dr. Joseph Boakye Danquah.•15 This
conference, as compared to previous protest
movements, was radical and nationalistic in
orientation. But in its "Seven Postulates", which
were greatly influenced by Dr. Danquah's work on
the conception of God in Akan philosophy,•16
almost nothing was said of political independence.
This was in striking contrast to the position of
the youth of Ghana a decade later. In 1948 the
Ghana Youth Manifesto addressed itself directly to
the political question:

> Youth of the Gold Coast, the new Ghana,
> the struggle for self-government gains
> unrelenting momentum, that brings us daily
> nearer our goal. However hard the struggle,
> whatever the stratagems of the imperialists,
> or whatever the opportunism of producers,
> stooges, and quislings to lead us astray, we
> shall not deviate an inch from our avowed
> goal.•17

We shall attempt to demonstrate that the
leaderships of these protests movements, with the
possible exception of the Ghana Youth Movement,
lacked a "mass-consensual orientation."•18

Professor Eisenstadt suggests that

> The consensual or mass aspect of modern
> society is rooted in the growing impingements
> of broader strata on the center, in their
> demands to participate in the sacred symbols
> of society and their formulation, and in the
> displacement of the traditional symbols by new

ones that stress these participatory and
social dimensions.•19

It must, however, be pointed out that though
the leadership of these movements had recognized
for some time the necessity for the masses to
"participate in the sacred symbols of society and
their formulation", as in the pamphlet presented
by the Gold Coast Youth Conference in 1938, •First
Steps Towards a National Fund•, the recognition of
this objective aspect of social change and
political development was blurred by the
subjectivist values of Dr. Danquah as demonstrated
in this interview with Richard Wright conducted in
1953:

Wright: Do   you   think (Nkrumah will) keep
power long?   Danquah: Yes, until   the
illiterate masses wake up. Wright: Why
don't you try to win the masses to
your side?

Danquah: Masses? I don't like this thing
of the   masses.   There   are   only
individuals for me.

Wright: But masses form the basis of
political   power in the modern
world today.

Danquah: You believe that?   I know you
fellows dote on this thing of the
masses....I've read that you claim that
this mass unrest comes from the
industrialization of the Western World.

Wright: Why is it that you cannot appeal to
the masses on the basis of their daily
needs?   You're a lawyer;You're used to
representing...Well, represent them.
As we say in America: be a mouthpiece
for them.

Danquah: I can't do things like that.

Wright: It's the only road to power in modern
society.   No matter how deeply you
reject it, it's true.

Danquah: It's emotion.20

Wright concluded, "He was shaking his head.
..It was no use. He was of the old school. One
did not speak •for• the masses; one •told• them
what to do...." The intellectual leadership of
the country, in their wish to identify with
Britain, as exemplified by this statement of
Professor Busia; "Oxford has made me what I am
today. I have had eleven years contact with it
and now consider it my second home. Most of my
friends are here (in England,"•21 "I'm a
Westerner and was educated in the West,"•22 He
tended to distrust and reject the masses. As
Cobina Kessie wrote in 1955:

When the masses act on their own, they
do so only in one way, for they have no
other: They lynch. It is not altogether by
chance that Mr. Nkrumah himself preached
"direct action" or "positive action" against
a previous government. For lynch law comes
from America, the paradise of the masses, and
Nkrumah was educated in America.23

Frantz Fanon sees in the national
consciousness of this intellectual leadership a
kind of symbiotic relationship with Britain -- the
intellectuals conceiving of themselves as the
political and cultural mediators between the
colonial administration and the traditional
rulers. Fanon refers to this consciousness as
national "bourgeois consciousness": "Seen through
its eyes, its mission has nothing to do with
transforming the nation; it consists prosaically
of being the transmission line between the
nation....and neo-colonialism."•24 But there were
other intellectuals who rejected their roles as
mediators between the colonial administration and
the traditional rulers and the people. In
rejecting this kind of symbiotic relationship with
Britain, they developed a "self-conscious neo-
traditionalism with anticolonial overtones".
Attoh Ahuma was perhaps the first advocate of this
neo-traditionalist consciousness. In 1911 he
hoped for "an era of Backward Movement" and
maintained that "Intelligent Retrogression is the
only Progression which will save our beloved
country", and echoed the need "to rid ourselves of
foreign accretions and excrescences" as a
precondition of "National Resurrection and
National Prosperity."•25

What Ghana needed was a movement with a
future orientation committed to a wholistic

ideology which would transform Gharaian society.
It was partially in response to this need that the
United Gold Coast Convention was formed, out of
which emerged the Convention People's Party.
While the U.G.C.C. aimed at a partial political
revolution, the C.P.P. aimed at a complete social
revolution. Marx, drawing the distinction between
a partial political revolution and a total social
revolution, put it this way:

> What is the basis of a partial, merely
> political revolution? Simply this: •a
> fraction of Civil society• emancipates itself
> and achieves a dominant position; a certain
> class undertakes, •from its particular
> situation,• a general emancipation of
> society, This class emancipates society as a
> whole, but only on condition that the whole
> of society is in the same situation as this
> class, for example, that it possesses or can
> acquire money or culture.26

To effect a total social transformation of
society, Marx opined that the class which forms
the basis of the ideological or wholistic
revolutionary movement must break away from the
past. This class, Marx argued, must be a class in
but not of the polity:

> A sphere of society which has a
> universal character because its sufferings
> are universal, and which does not claim a
> particular redress because the wrong which is
> done to it is not a particular wrong but
> wrong in general. There must be formed a
> sphere of society which claims no traditional
> status but only human status, a sphere which
> is not opposed to particular consequences but
> is totally opposed to the assumptions

We have provided this brief and analytical
background material on the evolution of
nationalism in Ghana in order to discuss and
analyze the Convention People's Party and its
programs in a more meaningful context. As we
shall see, the history of the evolution of
nationalism in Ghana greatly influenced the
formation of the C.P.P. and its program. And yet,
beyond these historical experiences, there also
developed many new characteristics which
constitute perhaps the unique character of the
C.P.P. as a party of national integration and a
vehicle for social change in Ghana. It would be

worth while to trace the evolution of the C.P.P.
and to analyze these characteristics.

NATIONALISM IN GESTATION

If the seeds of Ghanaian nationalism were
sown before the arrival of Nkrumah in Ghana after
twelve years of sojourn in the United States and
Britain, they matured with astonishing rapidity
after 1948. A number of variables explain this
phenomenal growth. First, during World War II,
the Allied Powers, Britain, France, and the United
States, had made sweeping promises to accelerate
the tempo of self-government for the colonial
peoples. Secondly, the thousands of Ghanaian
soldiers who had served overseas had broadened
their horizons and brought home with them new
ideas and skills which they had learned from the
Indian national struggle for independence, and
thirdly, war-time inflation and economic hardships
created discontent and inflamed grievances against
the colonial administration. The net result was
the emergence of group self-consciousness and an
awareness by the people of their plight under
colonialism and their desire to extricate
themselves from the chains of colonialism and
imperialism. This selfconsciousness and awareness
required an adjustment of existing social and
political attitudes. The struggle for political
independence was, for the first time, becoming a
reality.

How Africans reacted to the dominance of the
colonial administration has been vividly expressed
by Sithole of South Africa :
The emergent African nationalism, in
many ways, represents the degree to which the
white man's magic spell, which at the
beginning of the nineteenth century had been
cast on the African, is wearing off. As long
as this myth was thick and impenetrable, the
African adjusted himself as well as he could
to what he thought were gods, though gods
that ate corn. As long as the white man was
able to hold up his pretentions to the
African as real, the African was scared, and
never challenged the white man as his
national ruler. Alas, the externals have had
their day, and reality has taken its place;
but few white people in Africa realize this
extremely important change....A good part of
the present African generation....take the
white man as a matter of course....The white

man   can   no   longer   cast   his   spell   over
them....•28

THE UNITED GOLD COAST CONVENTION

Led   by   the   late   Dr.   Danquah,   the   United   Gold
Coast   Convention   was   formed   in   1946.   It   was
officially   inaugurated   in   August   1947.   The
U.G.C.C.   demanded   "self-government   for   the   peoples
of   the   Gold   Coast   at   the   earliest   opportunity".
The   movement   was   also   "to   insure   that   by   all
legitimate   and   constitutional   means   the   direction
and   control   of   Government   should   pass   into   the
hands   of   the   people   and   chiefs   in   the   shortest
possible   time."•29

Though   the   U.G.C.C.   was   a   nationalist
movement,   it   did   not   have   the   support   of   the
masses   for   it   was not a mass movement.   It also
lacked   internal   discipline   and   a   structure
characteristic   of   political   parties.   The U.G.C.C.
needed an organizer, someone who could devote   his
time   to   the tasks of the Convention.   It must be
pointed   out   that   most   of   the   members   of   the
Executive   Committee   of   the   U.G.C.C.   were   lawyers
and businessmen who were not particularly keen   to
relinquish   their   business   interests   and   enormous
legal   practice   for   the   cause   of   national
independence.   This   explains   why,   on   the
recommendations of Ako Adjei, Nkrumah, who was not
even   known   to   the leadership of the U.G.C.C.   was
accepted   as   the   national   organizer   of   the
Convention.•30   And   it   was   Nkrumah   who   really
politicized   the   Ghanaian   masses   and   worked   out   a
tactical   program   for   the   Working   Committee   of   the
Convention:

SHADOW CABINET

The   formation   of   a   Shadow   Cabinet   should
engage   the   serious   attention   of   the   Working
Committee   as   early   as   possible.   Membership
is   to   be   composed   of   individuals   selected   •ad
hoc•   to   study   the   jobs   of   the   various
ministries   that   would   be   decided   upon   in
advance   for   the   country   when   we   achieve   our
independence.   This   cabinet   will   forestall
any   unpreparedness   on   our   part   in   the
exigency of self-government being thrust upon
us   before   the   expected   time.

ORGANIZATIONAL WORK

The organizational work of implementing the platform of the Convention will fall into three periods:

FIRST PERIOD

a. Co-ordination of all the various organizations under the United Gold Coast Convention: i.e., apart from individual Membership of the various Political, Social, Educational, Farmers' and Women's Organizations as well as Native Societies, Trade Unions, Co-operative Societies, etc., should be asked to affiliate to the Convention.

b. The consolidation of branches already formed and the establishment of branches in every town and village of the country will form another major field of action during the first period.

c. Convention branches should be set up in each town and village throughout the colony, Ashanti, the Northern Territories and Togoland. The Chief or Odikro of each town or village should be persuaded to become the Patron of the Branch.

d. Vigorous Convention weekend schools should be opened whenever there is a branch of the Convention. The political mass education of the country for self-government should begin at these weekend schools.•31

SECOND PERIOD

To be marked by constant demonstrations throughout the country to test for organizational strength, making use of the political crises.

THIRD PERIOD

a. The convening of a Constitutional Assembly of the Gold Coast people to draw up the Constitution for self-government and National Independence.

b.   Organized   demonstration, boycott and
strike, our only weapons to support our
pressure for self-government.•32

What happens to society when people are
aroused by charismatic leaders to demand self-
government now?, and what happens to a people when
society is undergoing such a rapid change in
social and political attitudes? One possible
answer may be that in a time of rapid change in
social and political attitudes, the newly
politicized and aroused masses are forced to
determine for themselves how to work, how to live
and how to react to given circumstances. And in
this new awakening they remove themselves from a
sheltering and limiting environment into the
unknown wider horizons of a larger society.•33
And it was the creation of a tribally integrated
larger society that was the aim of the program
submitted by Nkrumah to the Working Committee of
the Convention. The main objective of this
program, it seems, was that in the process of mass
politicization the people would detach themselves
from old ethical values, challenge the validity of
the structure of external authority, i.e.,
colonialism, and once and for all extricate
themselves from the miasma of colonialism.

This is not an easy process. Inevitably it
involves a real crisis of doubt and searching for
a new experience and a new meaning of life.
People feel tensions in their physical and social
lives. But

Change itself is ethically neutral. In
the end it may be for the good of man and
society, but it destroys many values both old
and new.•34

THE INEVITABLE CONFRONTATION

It was Nkrumah's appreciation of the
ineluctable forces of social change and the lack
of appreciation and understanding of these forces
by the leadership of the United Gold Coast
Convention, that finally brought about the
inevitable confrontation leading to Nkrumah's
resignation from the U.G.C.C. The break was
inevitable because from the very beginning when
Nkrumah became the Organizing Secretary of the
U.G.C.C. he adopted revolutionary tactics unknown
in Ghanaian politics "to widen the membership and
to turn the U.G.C.C. into an active, popular

movement". The leadership of the U.G.C.C. adopted
a pragmatic and legalistic approach and engaged in
a sort of political bargaining and legal scheming.
Nkrumah, on the other hand, rejected this approach
and argued that "Imperialism knows no law beyond
its own interest and it is natural that despite
the pretensions of its agents to justice and fair
play, they always seek their interests first."
Nkrumah wrote in 1947, addressing the colonial
intellectuals:

> Those who formulate the colonial issue
> in accordance with the false point of view of
> colonial powers, who are deluded by the
> futile promises of 'preparing' colonial
> peoples for 'self-government', who feel that
> their imperialist oppressors are 'rational'
> and 'moral' and will relinquish their
> 'possessions' if only confronted with the
> truth of the injustice of colonialism are
> tragically mistaken.•35

This kind of symbiotic relationship with the
colonial power stems from type of education many
of the colonial intellectuals received from
metropolitan universities. Nkrumah analyzes the
defective approach to scholarship suffered by
different categories of colonial students as
follows:

> A colonial student does not by origin
> belong to the intellectual history in which
> the university philosophers are such
> impressive landmarks. The colonial student
> can be so seduced by these attempts to give a
> philosophical account of the universe, that
> he surrenders his whole personality to them.
> When he does this, he loses sight of the
> fundamental social fact that he is a colonial
> subject. In this way, he omits to draw from
> his education and from the concern displayed
> by the great philosophers for human problems,
> anything which he might relate to the very
> real problem of colonial domination, which,
> as it happens, conditions the immediate life
> of every colonized African.

> With single-minded devotion, the
> colonial student meanders through the
> intricacies of the philosophical systems.
> And yet, these systems did aim at providing a
> philosophical account of the world in the
> circumstances and conditions of their time.

For even philosophical systems are facts of
history. By the time, however, that they
come to be accepted in the universities for
exposition, they have lost the vital power
which they had at their first statement, they
have shed their dynamism and polemic
reference. This is a result of the academic
treatment which they are given. The academic
treatment is the result of an attitude to
philosophical systems as though there was
nothing to them but statements standing in
logical relation to one another.

This defective approach to scholarship
was suffered by different categories of
colonial students. Many of them had been
hand-picked and, so to say, carried
certificates of worthiness with them. These
were considered fit to become enlightened
servants of the colonial administration. The
process by which this category of student
became fit usually started at an early age,
for not infrequently they had lost contact
early in life with their traditional
background. By reason of their lack of
contact with their own roots, they became
prone to accept some theory of universalism,
provided it was expressed in vague,
mellifluous terms.

Armed with their universalism, they
carried away from their university courses an
attitude entirely at variance with the
concrete reality of their people and their
struggle. When they came across doctrines of
a combat nature, like those of Marxism, they
reduced them to arid abstractions, to common-
room subtleties. In this way, through the
good graces of their colonialist patrons,
these students, now competent in the art of
forming not a concrete environmental view of
social political problems, but an abstract,
"liberal" outlook, began to fulfill the hopes
and expectations of their guides and
guardians.

A few colonial students gained access to
metropolitan universities almost as of right,
on account of their social standing. Instead
of considering culture as a gift and a
pleasure, the intellectual who emerged
therefrom now saw it as a personal
distinction and privilege. He might have

suffered mild persecution at the hands of the
colonialists, but hardly ever really in the
flesh. From his wobbly pedestal, he indulged
in the history and sociology of his country,
and thereby managed to preserve some measure
of positive involvement with the national
process. It must however, be obvious that
the degree of national consciousness attained
by him was not of such an order as to permit
him full grasp of the laws of historical
development or of the thorough-going nature
of the struggle to be waged, if national
independence was to be won.

Finally, there were the vast number of
ordinary Africans, who, animated by a lively
national consciousness, sought knowledge as
an instrument of national emancipation and
integrity. This is not to say that these
Africans overlooked the purely cultural value
of their studies. But in order that their
cultural acquisition should be valuable, they
needed to be capable of appreciating it as
free men.

I was one of this number.•36

By temperament, training and philosophical
outlook, it was inevitable that Nkrumah was bound
to be at odds with the leadership of the U.G.C.C.
on strategy and tactics. As we shall see, the
difference between Nkrumah and the leadership of
the U.G.C.C. were brought into sharp focus after
the 1948 disturbances. The major difference was
philosophical. It revolved around the whole
question of decolonization and the organizational
method to be used in the process. This
fundamental difference would inevitably lead to
Nkrumah's resignation from the U.G.C.C.

On February 28, 1948, a petition was
addressed to the Governor by the Gold Coast Ex-
Service Men's Union, outlining their grievances
against the colonial government. In the petition,
the Union made the following points:

1.   Failure on the part of the Government to
      implement promises made to them while in
      the Army.

2.   Insufficiency of disablement pension
      rates having regard to the increased
      cost of living.

3.   That grants to men too old to enter
      Government Service and to men anxious to
      start business on their own account had
      not been made as was done in the United
      Kingdom.

4.   That provisions should be made exempting
      all ex-servicemen from payment of state
      levies for a period of five years.

5.   That army training in vocational work is
      not treated as adequate for civilian or
      Government employment of the same kind
      upon demobilization.

6.   That upon being demobilized and entering
      the Government service full   credit is
      not   given on establishment for the
      period of service in the army.

7.   That Africanization of the Royal West
      African Frontier Force was not being
      effectively maintained, and more African
      Officers should be granted regular
      commissions in the Army and non-
      commissioned officers should   be
      encouraged   to   take   the King's
      Commission. *37

The tragic events that followed the attempted
presentation of these grievances to the Governor
is recalled by Nkrumah in his autobiography. *38
But as conditions began to change, it became
necessary for the U.G.C.C. to take stock and
overhaul its entire political activity and its
method of organization. The entire arsenal was
reevaluated as an attempt to discard all that was
politically   antiquated,   and   to   revive the
movement. Without this re-examination, many
argued, it would be useless for the movement to
embark upon any confrontation with the colonial
government, and the movement would run the risk of
finding itself unprepared in the struggle for
political independence. This task required the
acceptance of responsibility for   one's   own
position and the taking of risks in working
towards political independence. It also required
a recognition of the fact that decolonization in
the political sense does not end on the day of the
attainment of political independence; that the
struggle for freedom*, in the full sense of the
word, begins on the day of political independence;
and that the removal of the colonial power may

create a vacuum which has to be filled with new
positive values.

The genuine task of this re-examination of
the political question fell to Kwame Nkrumah; and
finding himself at odds with the leadership of the
U.G.C.C., he tendered his resignation from the
U.G.C.C. on August 1, 1949. In his letter of
resignation he stated, inter alia:

> I am fully aware of the dangers to which
> I am thus exposed, but firm in the conviction
> that my country's cause comes first, I take
> the step and chance the consequences. I am
> prepared if need be to shed my blood and die
> if need be, that Ghana might have self-
> government now.•39

Interestingly enough, Nkrumah himself was not
aware of the differences between himself and the
leadership of the U.G.C.C. This became apparent
to him only after they had been thrown into jail.
Nkrumah relates this profound experience in his
autobiography:

> It was during this period when we were
> thrown together in such close proximity that
> I got the first indication of disagreement
> between myself and the other five members. I
> became painfully aware that they were losing
> interest in me because whenever we entered
> into a discussion, the five of them would
> always make a point of supporting the
> opposite point of view to mine and nothing I
> proposed was acceptable to them. There
> appeared to be a general belief among them
> that the whole tragedy of our arrest and
> suffering was my fault and they began to make
> it plain that they regretted the day they had
> ever invited me to take up the secretaryship
> of the U.G.C.C. Not satisfied with that,
> they even began to blame Ako Adjei for his
> part in recommending me to them.•40

With the resignation of Nkrumah from the
U.G.C.C. and the formation of the Convention
People's Party, began one of the most politicized
periods in the history of Ghana. In the next
chapter we shall examine briefly the formation of
the Convention People's Party.

REFERENCES

1.   Dr. James E.K. Aggrey was educated at
     Livingston College in Salisbury, N.C.
     and was Assistant Vice Principal of
     Prince of Wales' College, Achimota,
     Ghana.

2.   Edwin   W.   Smith, AGGREY OF AFRICA (New
     York, 1929), p.118.

3.   Kwame   Nkrumah, GHANA--The Autobiography
     of Kwame Nkrumah (London, 1965), pp. 12-
     13.

4.   We use the word "movements" because they
     were dependent on the personal interplay
     of individuals who were not subject to
     any   internal   discipline.   For   an
     excellent analysis of the difference
     between movements and political parties,
     see Maurice Duverger, POLITICAL PARTIES
     (New York, 1967).

     5. 1470-1471 is generally regarded as
the date of the first contact with the Gulf
of Guinea by
     Europeans.   But historians disagree on
     this date. Fage, for example, places
     the year between 1434-1482. The history
     of West Africa has been instructively
     examined by Professor F.D. Fage in AN
     INTRODUCTION TO THE HISTORY OF WEST
     AFRICA (Cambridge, England, 1961). For
     the beginning of European expansion in
     West Africa, see J.W. Blake, EUROPEAN
     BEGINNINGS IN WEST AFRICA, 1454-1578
     (London, 1937); and also by the same
     author, EUROPEANS IN WEST AFRICA, 1450-
     1650, I & II (Hakluyt Society, 1942).

6.   As quoted in G. Abednego Acquah, THE
     FANTSE   OF   GHANA   (Hull,   England,
     undated), pp. 45-46.

7.   For excellent historical surveys of the
     colonization process, see Sir Charles
     Lucas, THE PARTITION AND COLONIZATION OF
     AFRICA (Oxford, 1922), and Sir Harry
     Johnston,   THE   HISTORY   OF   THE
     COLONIZATION OF AFRICA BY ALIEN RACES
     (Cambridge, England, 1913).

38

8.   K.A. Busia, THE POSITION OF THE CHIEF IN
THE MODERN POLITICAL SYSTEM OF ASHANTI
(London, 1958), p. 42. This conception
of ancestral ownership of land is well
developed in the above book. See also
A. Allott, ESSAYS IN AFRICAN LAW
(London, 1960), I, pp. 153-307.

9   The Executive Members of the Confederacy
were: Nana Kwesi Edu, King of
Markession; Nana Otu, King of Abura;
J.H. Brew, Esq.; Chief Okyll of Cape
Coast; Honorable George Blankson, Jr.,
of Anomabu; J.E. Anissah, Esq. of
Abeadze Domisase; Rev. Joseph de Graft-
Hayford of Cape Coast; William Davidson,
Esq. of Kromantine; Francis Chapman
Grant and Jonah Myles Abadoo.

10.   Acquah, THE FANTSE OF GHANA, p. 56.

11.   The delegation was composed of : J.W.
Sey, President of the Society, George
Hughes, and T.F. Jones. The delegation
won the case against the Crown, and the
Crown Lands Bill was annulled. The
Society sent another delegation to
London in 1934 to seek a reform of the
Guggisberg Constitution and the
withdrawal of the Sedition and Water
Works Bills that had been passed by
Governor Sir Shenton Thomas. This
delegation was composed of Messrs.
George E. Moore and Samuel R. Wood.

12.   The founder of the West African Congress
was the late Casley Hayford. He was
author, journalist, barrister and
politician. He edited THE GOLD COAST
LEADER. Among his other works are
ETHIOPIA UNBOUND and GOLD COAST LAND
TENURE. The conference was held under
his guidance in 1917, Accra, Ghana.

13.   For a detailed account of the activities
of the West African Congress, see George
Padmore, GOLD COAST REVOLUTION (London,
1953). We must also point out that at
this time there were attempts by other
Black intellectuals in the 'Diaspora'
who were trying to deal with the
question of 'Black Liberation'. Among

these were Sylvester Williams, Marcus
Garvey and Dr. W.E.B. Dubois.

14.   For a sociological approach to the study
       of social movements, see S.N.
       Eisenstadt, MODERNIZATION: PROTEST AND
       CHANGE (Englewood Cliffs, N.J., 1966).
       See also the ff: H. Cantril, THE
       PSYCHOLOGY OF SOCIAL MOVEMENTS (New
       York, 1941); H. Kohn, "Pan-Movements",
       ENCYCLOPEDIA OF THE SOCIAL SCIENCES.
       (New York, 1933), XI, 544-554.

15.   Dr. Danquah, until his death, was the
       most respected intellectual in West
       Africa. He was also a strong opponent
       of Nkrumah and his policies. The Gold
       Coast Youth Conference had the support
       of Nana Sir Ofori Atta I, Omanhene of
       Kibi and a cousin of Dr. Danquah. This
       conference achieved practically nothing
       except for intellectual debates on the
       concept of state and nation, and the use
       of much more nationalistic rhetoric. On
       the question of race, a pamphlet
       published by the conference notes:
       "Neither the integrity nor ability nor
       the spirit for cooperation is wanting in
       the African. The youth of the country
       does not believe that these calumnies
       are true of the African as such, or of
       the European as such, for that matter.
       Individuals may prove themselves
       dishonest, incompetent, self-centered
       and vain not because they have so been
       brought up. Heredity alone is not
       responsible for what an individual turns
       out to be in society; environment counts
       for much, and the social milieu, and it
       is the duty of the country's leaders to
       improve the environment and the
       conditions of the social balance in
       which the growing child must weigh his
       future possibilities." From Youth
       Conference Pamphlet, FIRST STEPS TOWARDS
       A NATIONAL FUND (Achimota, 1938), quoted
       in David E. Apter, GHANA IN TRANSITION
       (New York, 1963), p. 128.

16.   The concept of God in Akan philosophy is
       exhaustively discussed by Dr. Danquah in
       AKAN LAW AND CUSTOMS; AKAN DOCTRINE OF
       GOD.

17. GHANA YOUTH MANIFESTO (Accra, 1948), quoted in Apter, GHANA IN TRANSITION, p. 15.

18. This concept is discussed by Professor E. Shils in "The Theory of Mass Society", DIOGENES, XXXIX (1963), 45-66, cited in Eisenstadt, MODERNIZATION, p. 15.

19. IBID., p. 15.

20. Richard Wright, BLACK POWER--A record of Reactions in a Land of Pathos (New York, 1954), pp. 220-221.

21. As quoted in MONTHLY REVIEW, XVIII (July-August, 1966), p.62.

22. IBID., p. 64 (For an analysis of the background of the colonial elites, see pp. 25-26).

23. ASHANTI PIONEER (January 26, 1955), Mr. Cobina Kessie was later appointed by Nkrumah as Ghana's Ambassador to the People's Republic of China.

24. Frantz Fanon, WRETCHED OF THE EARTH (New York, 1964), p.124.

25. As quoted in David Kimble, A POLITICAL HISTORY OF GHANA, 1850-1928 (Oxford, 1963), pp. 449-501.

26. Karl Marx, KRITIK DES HEGELSCHEN STAATRECHTS, translated in KARL MARX: SELECTED WRITINGS, edited by T.B. Bottomore (New York, 1964), p. 179.

27. IBID., p. 182. For other non-Marxian analyses of the processes of social change, see the following for an explication of this exceedingly complicated and diffuse process: Talcot Parsons, "Some Considerations on the Theory of Social Change", RURAL SOCIOLOGY, 26, Sept. 1961, pp. 220-234; M. Levy, THE STRUCTURE OF SOCIETY (Princeton, Princeton University Press, 1952); George K. Zollschan and Walter Hirsch, eds., EXPLORATIONS IN SOCIAL CHANGE (Boston: Houghton Mifflin, 1964);

and the most comprehensive sociological
treatment of revolutions by Pitirim A.
Sorokin, THE SOCIOLOGY OF REVOLUTION
(Philadelphia: J.B. Lippincott, 1925);
and also Everett E. Hagen ON THE THEORY
OF SOCIAL CHANGE, (Homewood, ILL.: The
Dorsey Press, 1962). I must point out
that a fundamental dilemma in the
modernization process is whether to opt
for rapid political development or rapid
economic development and pay the price
of the erosion of social cohesion. For
an excellent analysis of this dilemma
faced by the elites of the transitional
societies see "Economic, Social, and
Political Development in the
Underdeveloped Countries", a report
prepared by a group of scholars at the
Center of International Studies of the
Massachusetts Institute of Technology
for and published pursuant to Sen. Res.
336, 85th Congress, and Sen. Res. 31,
86th Congress, March 1960; U.S.
Government Printing Office, Washington
D.C.

28.   Ndabaningi Sithole, AFRICAN NATIONALISM
(Cape Town, 1959), pp. 146-147.

29.   For a complete account of the activities
of the U.G.C.C., see Apter, GHANA IN
TRANSITION, pp. 167-172. See also Kwame
Nkrumah, GHANA--THE AUTOBIOGRAPHY OF
KWAME NKRUMAH, pp. 64-101; Dennis
Austin, POLITICS IN GHANA (London,
1964); George Padmore, THE GOLD COAST
REVOLUTION (London, 1953); David Kimble,
A POLITICAL HISTORY OF GHANA 1850-1928
(Oxford, 1963).

30.   Nkrumah, GHANA, p. 61.

31.   We shall see later on that he created
the post of Education Secretary in the
Convention People's Party and
subsequently established the Ideological
Institute to further the party's aims.

32.   Nkrumah, GHANA, pp. 71-72.

33.   For a sociological and anthropological
interpretation of the process of rapid
social change in Asia, Africa and South

42

America, see Egbert DeVries, MAN IN
RAPID SOCIAL CHANGE (Garden City, New
York, 1961).

34. IBID., p. 101. "The Feeling of freedom
is essential to all human endeavor and
the promise of freedom one of the most
powerful agents in social change." p.
239.

35. Kwame Nkrumah, TOWARDS COLONIAL FREEDOM
(London, 1962), p. xiv.

36. Kwame Nkrumah, CONSCIENCISM: PHILOSOPHY
AND IDEOLOGY FOR DECOLONIZATION AND
DEVELOPMENT WITH PARTICULAR REFERENCE TO
THE AFRICAN REVOLUTION (London, 1964),
pp. 2-4.

37. Report of the Watson Commission (Accra,
1948).

38. Nkrumah, GHANA, pp. 75-87. As the Ex-
Servicemen's Union staged their peaceful
march to the castle to present their
petition to the Governor, they were met
at the Christiansburg cross-roads and
ordered to retreat. When they refused,
the colonial Police Officer,
Superintendent Imray, ordered the
African policemen to open fire on the
ex-servicemen. The African policemen
hesitated, and Superintendent Imray
himself fired into the marchers, killing
three of the leaders of the ex-
servicemen. When the news reached
greater Accra that Sgt. Adjeity had been
killed by a white man, people started
rioting and looting of all European
stores. The rioting and looting spread
all over the country and it took almost
two weeks for the colonial government to
put an end to the riots and looting.
Subsequently, the "Big Six" (Nkrumah,
Danquah, Akufu-Addo, O. Lamptey, Ofori
Ata) were arrested and detained for
sparking the disorders. *Freedom in
this sense is defined as the right of
the new political elites to restructure
the infrastructure of society and to
create new normative values for the new
social order to replace the colonial
system.

39.   IBID., pp. 102-109.

40.   IBID., p. 82.

THE CONVENTION PEOPLE'S PARTY

> In all political struggles there
> come rare moments, hard to distinguish but
> fatal to let slip, when all must be set upon
> a hazard, and out of the simple man is
> ordained strength.
> Kwame Nkrumah, 1949

The process of decolonization has been characterized not only by the continuous change in attitudes toward foreign authority, but also the breakdown of traditional authority, and of the self-sufficiency and independence of different tribal groups and strata as they were drawn toward a more unified, institutional order and the center of the polity. The various sub-groups, be they tribal, kinship groups or traditional institutional bodies, were drawn together into a common organizational framework, the Party. Some of the more traditional ascriptive criteria of status, be they tribal, estate, or kinship ones, were broken down and somewhat more flexible and variegated social strata emerged. Status now was attained through educational, occupational, and political channels. New forms of social organization, ranging from various functionally specific economic enterprises to various civic and voluntary associations also emerged. Hence, although these changes in society usually opened up new perspectives of advancement and change in social and economic status, advancement also became a focus of insecurity and political conflict as the history of the Convention People's Party well dramatizes.

The issues leading to the inevitable confrontation between Nkrumah and the leadership of the United Gold Coast Convention is narrated in Nkrumah's autobiography.[1] Before submitting his letter of resignation, he wrote:

> I was confronted by an excited crowd. "Resign!" they shouted, as soon as they saw me, "resign and lead us and we shall complete the struggle together!"

> I realized at once that they were sincere and determined. Above all I knew

they needed me to lead them. I had stirred
their deepest feelings and they had shown
their confidence in me; I could never fail
them now. Quickly I made up my mind.

"I will lead you!" I said. "This very
day I will lead you!"

Hurriedly I returned to the conference
room and announced that I had decided to
resign, not only from the Secretaryship, but
also from the membership of the U.G.C.C. The
delegates were then as jubilant as the crowd
outside. Standing on the platform surrounded
by an expectant crowd, I asked for a pen and
a piece of paper, and using somebody's back
as support, I wrote out my official
resignation and then read it to the people.
The reaction was immediate and the cheers
were deafening...Standing before my
supporters, I pledged myself, my very life
blood, if need be, to the cause of Ghana.•2

Nkrumah claims that a lady supporter of his
led the crowd in singing LEAD KINDLY LIGHT as he
wept and covered his eyes. This hymn was to
become the official hymn of the Convention
People's Party.

Nkrumah's resignation took place on July 30,
1949. But before this date, on June 12, 1949, he
had already launched the Convention People's Party
at the Accra West End Arena, with the slogan
"Self-Government Now" and with these mottoes: "We
prefer SelfGovernment With Danger to Servitude in
Tranquility"; "We Have the Right to Live as Men";
and "We Have the Right to Govern Ourselves".

The membership of the C.P.P., while generally
younger, more militant, and less affluent, did
not, however, reject the traditional values of
Ghanaian society, although it questioned them and
aimed at changing them. Less affluent and less
well established in society, the C.P.P. was not
able to utilize non-institutional channels of
reform. It attempted to use non-violent positive
action to exert pressure on the colonial
government. To achieve its stated objectives, the
C.P.P. had to steer its course between the
position of the U.G.C.C. and that of the colonial
government. Any other tactics would cost the
C.P.P. the mass support it needed and would
possibly have caused a split in the leadership.

The pragmatic approach of the C.P.P.'s willingness to work within the colonial institutional framework can be seen in its first Six Point Program. It was with this program that Nkrumah launched the C.P.P.:

1. To fight relentlessly by all constitutional means for the achievement of full "Self-Government Now" for the chiefs and people of the Gold Coast.

2. To serve as the vigorous conscious political vanguard for removing all forms of oppression and for the establishment of a democratic government.

3. To secure and maintain the complete unity of the chiefs and people of the colony, Ashanti, Northern Territories and Trans-Volta.

4. To work in the interest of the trade union movement in the country for better conditions of employment.

5. To work for a proper reconstruction of a better Gold Coast in which the people shall have the right to live and govern themselves as free people.

6. To assist and facilitate in any way possible the realization of a united and self-governing West Africa.•3

The Labour Government in Britain regarded this Six PointProgram with unqualified approbation--as long as the C.P.P.'s fight was within "constitutional means". As long as the vanguard aim of the party was such unqualified goals as "democracy", "unity", and "a better Gold Coast in which the people shall have the right to live and govern themselves as free people"; and as long as the perspective of the party for the working men was not the "proletarian take over of society" but for "better conditions of employment", the Labour Government was willing to deal with the C.P.P.

The pragmatism of the C.P.P. was tested when the Coussey Commission's Report•4 came out in October, 1949. The Report provided for the following institutional structure: The creation of strong municipal councils in Accra, Sekondi-

Takoradi, Cape Coast and Kumasi; local councils
and Upper House responsive to the interest of the
chiefs and traditional rulers in the country; an
Executive Council to be responsible for Government
policy and direct the administration of the
country. The elected African members were to be
in the majority in the Executive Council with the
exception of the three ex-officio members
appointed by the Crown. These three members were
to be responsible for the portfolios of Defense
and External Affairs, Justice, and Finance with
the Governor as Chairman of the Council.
Territorially, the chiefs were to be represented
through their elected representatives from the
Provincial Council of Chiefs. Mining and
commercial interests were also given special
seats.

Other recommendations in the Report were: (a)
Thirty-three rural members to be elected in two
stages, first by direct primary voting, and
secondly through electoral colleges in the Colony
and Ashanti; (b) nineteen members representing the
inhabitants of the Northern Territories, the
election to be conducted through specially
constituted electoral colleges. The
municipalities were to be represented by five
members, two from Accra and one each from Kumasi,
Sekondi-Takoradi and Cape Coast, and the elections
were to be conducted by direct voting based on
universal adult suffrage.

The C.P.P. was faced with a dilemma. The
Coussey Report provided for a governmental
structure which would not bring about an
institutional transfer of power to the people.
Should the party accept the report as a temporary
setback and continue to work within the
institutional framework? Or should it adopt a
militant posture? Nkrumah accepted the latter and
denounced the Report as a "Trojan gift horse" and
as "bogus and fraudulent" and called for "positive
action" to be staged.•5 And in a resolution
passed by the Ghana Representative Assembly
convened by the C.P.P. on November 20, 1949, the
Assembly stated in effect:

The Coussey Report and His Majesty's
Government Statement thereon are unacceptable
to the country as a whole and that the people
of the Gold Coast be granted Dominion Status
within the Commonwealth of Nations based on
the Statute of Westminster.

While the above resolution was being passed,
Nkrumah entered into negotiations with Sir Arden-
Clarke, the Governor, and Regional Saloway, the
Colonial Secretary, to liberalize the proposals of
the Coussey Commission's Report. It seemed that
an orderly process of colonial devolution was
going to be worked out. But the activism of the
politicized and awakened masses forced Nkrumah to
abandon the negotiations. Nkrumah himself may
have been partially responsible for the militancy
of the masses. "Get ready, people of the Gold
Coast", he told his followers at the Accra West
End Arena on December 15, "the era of positive
action draws nigh."•6 Nkrumah gave the Colonial
Government two weeks to accept the demands of the
C.P.P. The stage was set for the inevitable
confrontation with the Colonial Government. The
Ghana Trades Union Congress began to prepare the
grand strategy for a general strike, and the urban
masses were prepared for a boycott of European
shops.

Nkrumah himself seemed not to have been
prepared for this confrontation. Just as
preparations were being carried out for the
confrontation, several meetings took place between
Nkrumah, Sir Arden-Clarke and Secretary Saloway.
The C.P.P.'s newspaper, the Evening News, twice
announced that positive action would be postponed,
and at one time Nkrumah called it off. That
Nkrumah was not prepared for positive action is
attested to by Saloway's version of the events of
these critical days :

Nkrumah publicly called off "positive
action" and tried hard to get the Trade Union
Congress to call off the strike, but the
T.U.C. no longer had any control over the
wild men. (Moreover) Dr. Danquah taunted
Nkrumah with having sold himself to the
Colonial Secretary and thus infuriated the
rank and file of the C.P.P. who forced
Nkrumah to retract.•7

And Sir Arden-Clarke adds:

The party leaders had been officially
informed and were well aware that they had a
perfectly constitutional way of achieving
power and gaining their objective if their
candidates at the forthcoming election were
returned. I have good reason to believe that
some at least of the party leaders would have
preferred not to resort to "positive action"

but to await the results of the general
election, the outcome of which they were
fairly confident. But they found themselves
enmeshed in the coils of their own
propaganda. The tail wagged the dog.•8

By January 6, 1950, the T.U.C. forced the
issue by calling for a general strike. Nkrumah
was now forced to take a stand-to side either with
the colonial government or with the T.U.C.   On
January 8, he announced his party's support for
the T.U.C. and sparked positive action, which
would "take the form of a simple and fundamentally
spiritual exercise."•9

The Colonial Government, declaring the
general strike illegal, arrested the leadership of
the T.U.C. and the C.P.P. and charged them with
sedition and coercing the colonial government and
of calling an illegal strike. They were tried and
sentenced. In spite of their imprisonment, the
C.P.P. did not lose support. Rather, it began to
gather a wider mass following.   Just two months
after their trials, municipal elections were held
in Accra, the capital of the country. The C.P.P.
won all the seats and defeated the candidates of
the U.G.C.C. It thus became crystal clear to Sir
Arden-Clarke that the C.P.P. was the most popular
political party in the country. The position of
the colonial government in relation to the C.P.P.
was summarized by Sir Arden-Clarke as follows:

Nkrumah and his party had the mass of
the people behind them and there was no other
party with appreciable public support to
which one could turn. Without Nkrumah, the
Constitution would be stillborn and if
nothing came of all the hopes, aspirations,
and concrete proposals for the greater
measure of self-government, there would no
longer be any faith in the good intentions of
the British Government and the Gold Coast
would be plunged into disorders, violence and
bloodshed.10

Given these circumstances, the colonial
government had no meaningful choice but to release
Nkrumah to contest the 1951 general election.•11
Out of the 38 popularly contested seats, the
C.P.P. won 34 with vast majorities.•12

The C.P.P. manifesto of 1951, entitled
"Towards the Goal", put forth the following
objectives:

1. Constitutional: The Coussey Committee let the country down by prolonging white imperialism.•13 The C.P.P. will fight for self-government NOW.

2. Political: An Upper House of the Legislature, known as the Senate, shall be created for the Chiefs. Universal suffrage at the age of 21. Direct elections with no property or residential qualifications for candidates.

3. Economic: A Five Year Economic Plan...

   (i)   Immediate materialization of the Volta hydroelectric scheme.

   (ii)   Railway lines to be doubled and extended.

   (iii) Roads to be modernized and extended.

   (iv)   Canals to join rivers.

   (v)   Progressive mechanizaticn of t+1

   (v)   Progressive mechanizaticn of agriculture.
   (vi)   Special attention will be given to the swollen shoot disease;   farmers will be given control of the
          Cocoa Industry Board Funds...

4. Social: Education.

   (i) A unified system of free compulsory elementary, secondary, and technical education up to 16 years of age.

   (ii) The University College to be brought up to University status.

   (iii)   A planned campaign to abolish illiteracy.

5. Family Assistance:

   (i) A free national health service.

   (ii) A high standard housing program...

(iii) A piped-water supply in all parts of
the country...

(iv) A national insurance scheme.

The five year economic plan of the party's
1951 manifesto, in essence, reflected the main
provisions of the "Ten Year Plan" of 1951, which
had been submitted by Sir Arden-Clarke. The
Party's economic platform was at best reformist.
There was nothing revolutionary about it that
might have given the Colonial Government second
thoughts. The revolutionary rhetoric of the
campaign was at variance with the party's
manifesto. The activists within the Trade Union
Congress attempted to form a Labor Party, but
nothing concrete materialized.

How did the Ghanaian masses react to the
party's manifesto of gradualism and to what extent
were they politically activated by Nkrumah's call
for independence NOW? On the basis of the 1951
general election returns, two deductions are
possible. The first deduction is that the C.P.P.
was a mass party and had more popular support than
the U.G.C.C. The C.P.P. won 34 of the 38
popularly contested seats. The second deduction
is that the majority of the masses was indifferent
to the C.P.P. manifesto. Despite intensive
campaigning by both the C.P.P. and the U.G.C.C.
and the efforts of the Colonial Government to have
people register, only about forty percent of the
eligible electorate registered.

NUMBER OF REGISTERED VOTERS 1951•14

Area	Estimated Population	Eligible Electorate	Registered Voters	
			Number	Per Cent
Colony (incl.S. Togoland)	2,153,310	1,095,190	350,525	32.0
Ashanti	784,210	398,590	220,658	55.4
Municipalities	290,230	141,480	90,275	64.1
TOTAL	3,227,750	1,635,260	661,458	40.5

What happened after 1951? Why did the C.P.P.
which seemed so confident and successful at the

1951 general elections, falter, until it seemed to
have reached a point of collapse when faced with
the political organization of the Right-regional,
religious and tribal elements? And why did the
C.P.P. after the 1951 elections turn to full
cooperation with the Colonial Government in order
to achieve "self-government NOW"?

There are several reasons. The most obvious
is that the apparent victories of the C.P.P. at
the 1951 elections did not bring about any degree
of change in the lives of the people. The
inadequacy of the C.P.P. manifesto is not
difficult to grasp. It failed even to mention the
urban workers or the farmers. Even the most
superficial analysis of the changes that occurred
between 1951 and 1966 shows the connection between
hopes raised by the C.P.P. leadership and the
masses' disappointing realization that the C.P.P.,
whatever its apparent successes at the polls,
failed nevertheless to relieve the tangible
evidences of colonial life.

Not only did the platform of the C.P.P. prove
to be intrinsically weaker and limited in its
application than seemed possible after the 1951
elections, but the unexpectedly bitter resistance
to "self-government NOW" and national integration
by the Right opposition, particularly in Ashanti,
made it difficult for the C.P.P. to implement even
its limited reformist objectives. The strategy of
the C.P.P., resting implicitly on the assumption
that the colony was more politicized and
enlightened than Ashanti and the Northern
Territories, was unprepared for the resistance it
encountered in Ashanti and the Northern
Territories.

The shifting focus of the C.P.P. from "self-
government NOW" to national unity contributed to
the weakening of the C.P.P. in Ashanti, the
Northern Territories and Trans-Volta Togoland
Region. The implications of this shift of focus
go beyond what was immediately evident--that the
colonial Government appeared to be on the side of
the Right opposition. It was at this time that
the former Governor of India, Sir Frederic Bourne,
was sent to Ghana by the British Government to
help solve the crisis. A Constitutional
Commission was set up to examine the claims of the
various parties and to draw up a constitution
suited to Ghana. The Right opposition boycotted
the Commission. In December 1955, Sir Frederic
published his report which fell short of

federalism. In his report, he recommended the
setting up of Regional Assemblies for the
following reasons: (a) to avoid over-
centralization; (b) to obtain local opinion on
matters of national importance; (c) to adopt
legislative and Government activity to regional
needs. The fears of the Right opposition that the
over-politicized and enlightened South would
dominate the rest of the country were not abated
by the Bourne Report. In the proposal put forth
by the "Movements and Parties other than the
Convention People's Party" a peculiar statement
appeared indicative of sophisticated self-
conscious tribalism:

> The peoples of these territories,
> belonging as they do to different tribes,
> have different structures of society, and are
> at different stages of adaptation and
> adoption of Western culture....There is not
> enough consciousness of national identity to
> make possible easy and at the same time
> democratic unitary government. In the
> absence of this consciousness, the safest
> course is to ensure that not all the powers
> of government are concentrated at the center
> but that a substantial part of them is
> retained in the component territories where
> people have learned the habits and attitudes
> of living together for some time.•15

The emergence of the Right Opposition (the
traditional rulers), particularly in Ashanti and
the Northern Territories, was the product of a set
of conditions; C.P.P. efforts to "destool" Chiefs
unsympathetic to its cause; the tendency of the
C.P.P. leadership to emasculate chieftancy and the
tendency of the intellectuals to express their
distaste for the C.P.P. vicariously by attacking
Nkrumah, rather than by confronting the issues.
Moreover, the strength of C.P.P. in the Colony
rested on the urban workers, who by migrating to
the cities were not able to transplant their
tribal way of life, in contrast to their tribal
counterparts in Ashanti and the North who
maintained their semi-autonomous tribal way of
life, therefore giving its own distinctive mark to
the Right Opposition. In the rural areas of
Ashanti and the North, the Chiefs implanted an
ethic of patience, suffering, and endurance. This
kind of ethic proved conducive to the separatist
movements of the Right Opposition--once endurance
was divested from apathy to political activism.
But this kind of ethic did not long survive the
exposure to Southern affluence and materialism.

54

It soon gave way to an ethic of materialism and accumulation. But in those areas of the country where the ethic of materialism and accumulation did not particularly thrive, especially in Ashanti, it gave way to violence and hatred for the C.P.P.•16

This analysis in turn makes it possible to see why the Right Opposition, which never made much headway in the Colony, found Ashanti and the Northern Territories a fertile soil; while the C.P.P. , on the other hand, became progressively weaker in these two areas of the country as the focus of the struggle shifted from "self-government NOW" to national integration, as shown by the results of the 1956 general elections.

NUMBER OF SEATS WON BY THE POLITICAL PARTIES

Convention People's Party........... 71

National Liberation Movement....... 16

Northern People's Party............ 12

Togoland Congress Party............ 2

Ghana Congress Party.............. 1

Moslem Association Party........... 1

Anlo Youth Organization............ 1

TOTAL.......... 104

In Ashanti the C.P.P. won six out of twenty-one seats; in the Northern Territories, it won eleven seats out of twenty-six; and in Togoland eight out of thirteen. It won every seat in the Colony.

With this showing of mass support, the inevitable was to happen. On September 17, 1956, Nkrumah was summoned to the Governor's residence and handed a despatch from the Secretary of State for the Colonies fixing March 6, 1957, as the date for independence. Thus centuries of protest

finally culminated in political independence with
the C.P.P. as the most important party in Ghana.

Concerning the revolutionary spirit of the
C.P.P. for social transformation and political
change, Nkrumah was not certain. How best could
the party that led the struggle for political
independence be transformed into an instrument for
the social transformation of society? From the
point of view of Nkrumah, the question was not
whether the C.P.P. as a mass-based party should be
strengthened, but whether the party under his sole
and undisputed leadership could become a historic
agent of social change. And as he put it himself:

As a ship that has been freshly launched
we face the hazards of the high seas alone.
We must rely on our own men, on the captain
and on his navigation. And, as I proudly
stand on the bridge of that lone vessel as
she confidently sets sail, I raise a hand to
shade my eyes from the glaring African sun
and scan the horizon. There is so much
beyond.17

After independence, it had become clear to
Nkrumah that at a time of vast and impersonal
political and social change a well defined
revolutionary leadership would make a difference
in a society such as Ghana. It devolved on
Nkrumah to introduce purposive, conscious, and
responsive intervention in Ghana's political and
social revolution. To effect this, Nkrumah
decided to create groupings of able individuals
who would systematically generate in the polity
the creative social and political innovations that
were needed to rally the masses behind the C.P.P.
to carry on the social transformation of Ghana.

What the C.P.P. leadership realized was that
it was impossible to wield power, or to exercise
it effectively, and more especially to use it
actively, unless there was some sharing of certain
values, implicitly or overtly, among the party
activists and the masses. Thus ideological
training became a vital aspect of the activities
of the C.P.P. after independence. As we shall see
later in Chapter Three, Nkrumah felt that the
party, in leading the struggle for socialism,
should provide its members with a sense of
consistency and certainty. In essence, the party
activists were required to ponder these questions:

t--t 1. hat is the real meaning of our
historical epoch in Ghana and Africa?

2.   What are the motive forces changing reality in our lifetime?

3.   How can we best relate ourselves to those changes so that the Party would successfully lead the struggle, ideologically, for socialism?

In order to effect the C.P.P.'s Programme for Work and Happiness, i.e., the socialist program of the party, the party needed socialists. As Nkrumah put it to the C.P.P. Study Group in Accra on April 22, 1961:

We cannot build Socialism without Socialists and we must take positive steps to ensure that the Party and the country produce the men and women who can handle a Socialist Programme.

This, in turn, necessitated the introduction of an ideology and party ideological education. It is this ideology--Nkrumaism--which we shall examine in Chapter Three to provide us with the basis of analyzing and understanding the impact of the Programme for Work and Happiness on Ghana.

REFERENCES

1.   See also Apter, GHANA IN TRANSITION; Dennis Austin, POLITICS IN GHANA. (London, 1964); Padmore, THE GOLD COAST REVOLUTION.

2.   Nkrumah, GHANA, p. 107.

3.   Ibid., p. 101.

4.   See Report of His Excellency, the Governor by the Committee on Constitutional Reform, 1949, Colonial No. 248 (Coussey Commission).

5.   Nkrumah defined "positive action" as the "adoption of all legitimate and constitutional means by which we could attack the forces of imperialism in the country. The weapons were legitimate political agitation, newspaper and

history was the coming together for the first time of the Northern Territories, Ashanti and the Colony under one central administration in 1946 under the "Eurns Constitution". Hitherto, the Northern Territories, a protectorate, and Ashanti, which had been conquered by the British in 1900, were administered separately. It was only in 1946 that the three regions came together under one central legislature.

16.   These observations rest on Apter's work, GHANA IN TRANSITION.

17.   Nkrumah, GHANA, p. 290.

educational campaigns and, as a last
resort, the constitutional application
of strikes, boycotts, and non-
cooperation based on the principle of
absolute non-violence, as used by
Ghandi". GHANA, pp. 111-112.

6. EVENING NEWS (Accra, Ghana, December
16, 1949).

7. Saloway, INTERNATIONAL AFFAIRS
(October 1955), p. 47.

8. Charles Arden-Clarke, "Eight Years in
the Gold Coast", AFRICAN AFFAIRS
(January 1958), p. 50. Also ASHANTI
PIONEER (January 7, 1950).

9. ASHANTI PIONEER (January 7, 1950).
The T.U.C. (Trade Union Congress) is the
national organization of labor unions in
Ghana. It provided much of the support
and the organizational skills the C.P.P.
needed in its infancy. It subsequently
became the industrial wing of the
C.P.P.

10. Arden-Clarke, AFRICAN AFFAIRS (January
1958) as quoted in Austin, POLITICS IN
GHANA, p. 150.

11. For a discussion of the campaign and
electoral politics, see Nkrumah, GHANA,
p. 133; and Austin, POLITICS IN GHANA,
pp. 103-152.

12. For an analysis of the election, see
Kenneth Robinson and W.J. MacKenzie,
FIVE AFRICAN ELECTIONS (Oxford, 1960).

13. This was the first time the term "white
imperialism" was used in Ghanaian
politics.

14. Taken from Austin, POLITICS IN GHANA,
p. 113.

15. "Preamble Proposals for a Federal
Constitution for an Independent Gold
Coast and Togoland by Movements and
Parties other than the Convention
People's Party" (Kumasi, undated).
Cited in Austin, POLITICS IN GHANA, p.
277. It must be pointed out that an
important historical landmark in Ghana's

NKRUMAISM AS A NATIONAL IDEOLOGY

Before examining Nkrumaism as a national
ideology, we must indicate why Nkrumaism is a
unique phenomenon to Ghanaian politics and then
try to define the term. Nkrumaism as an ideology
is unique in Ghanaian politics because for the
first time a political leader in a position of
power attempted to institutionalize his own
philosophical frame of thought by establishing an
institution whose main task was to disseminate and
propagate Nkrumaism.

What, then, is Nkrumaism? Nkrumaism is the
"scientific" application of the "original humanist
principles underlying African society" and the
"African experience of Islamic and Euro-Christian
presence...and, by gestation, (it) employ(s) them
for the harmonious growth and development of that
society".1 Nkrumaism, in essence, "is the map in
intellectual terms of the disposition of forces
which will enable African society to digest the
Western and the Islamic and Euro-Christian
elements in Africa, and develop them in such a way
that they fit into the African personality".2

We must note here, that Nkrumaism as an
ideology is not restricted to Ghana, but is to be
applied to the developmental process in Africa as
a whole.

Nkrumah, it may be postulated, saw soon after
independence that the winning of political
independence was not an end in itself but "a means
to the economic and social emancipation of the
nation and the people."3 Political independence
is the beginning of the second revolution--the
economic and social revolution. But after
independence, "There were also certain individuals
who, having satisfied themselves with the personal
gains they derived from the first revolution,
found it difficult and were unwilling to move
forward with the second revolution of economic and
social reconstruction that will bring upliftment
and advancement to the wider masses of the
people."4

The second phase of the revolution, from the
point of view of Nkrumah, could not be carried out
without a transvaluation of national

consciousness. In the absence of a cultural
ethos--the characteristic spirit of a community-
transvaluation of national consciousness was
impossible without the introduction of a
nationally acceptable ideology. It is, perhaps,
the greatest achievement of Nkrumah to have
clarified this point and to have tried to
actualize his theoretical framework. He embraced
the idea that Nkrumaism would be accepted and
understood by every stratum of Ghanaian society
within a single generation. To him, the content
of Nkrumaism coincided in substance with the triad
of Ghanaian experience i.e., Islamic experience,
Euro-Christian experience, and the traditional
African experience.5 In effect, Nkrumah has
argued that

> Since society implies a certain dynamic
> unity, there needs to emerge an ideology
> which, genuinely catering for the needs of
> all, will take the place of the competing
> ideologies, and so reflect the dynamic unity
> of society, and be the guide to society's
> continual progress.6

This triad of Ghanaian experience may be
represented graphically as follows:

Triad of Ghanaian Experience

1. Thesis---Traditional   Tribalism
            African   Ethnic Loyalty
            Experience   Regionalism

2. Antithesis--Islamic   Religion-Islam
               Experience Slavery

         Euro-Christian Religion-
            Experience   Christianity
                             Slavery
                             Colonialism
                             Imperialism

3. Synthesis--NKRUMAISM   Independence
                             Freedom &
                          Justice
                             Equality of
                             Opportunity

         Legitimacy

Authority

Political Stability

Social Justice

The synthesis was presented as the new
ideology and was suggestively descriptive of the
process of colonization and decolonization. The
thesis and antithesis are references to instances
of what Ghanaians experienced under traditionalism
and the Islamic and Euro-Christian influences.
When an actual occasion (foreign domination and
traditionalism) is past, Nkrumah has argued, it
continues to have a sort of mythical actuality in
society. But this actuality is no longer that of
a living reality. The new actuality is now
NKRUMAISM--the national ideology.7

Speaking before the party activists at the
first two-day Party Seminar at the Kwame Nkrumah
Institute of Ideological Studies at Winneba, held
on the 3rd and 4th of February, 1962, Nkrumah
called on the party activists to carry forward
party education to the masses and provide them
with the necessary knowledge to understand the
painful process of nation building.8 The he went
on to outline the nature of the vehicle to be used
in this process, i.e., the ideology of Nkrumaism:

> The Party has defined a social purpose
> and it is committed to socialism and to the
> ideology of Nkrumaism, and I take it to mean
> that when you talk of Nkrumaism, you mean the
> name or term given to the consistent
> ideological policies followed and taught by
> Kwame Nkrumah. These are contained in
> speeches, in his theoretical writings and
> stated ideas and principles. You also mean
> that Nkrumaism, in order to be Nkruma-istic,
> must be related to scientific socialism. To
> be successful, however, this ideology must:
>
> a)   Be all-pervading, and while its theories
>   in full can only be developed in and
>   around the Party leadership, it must
>   influence in some form all education
>   and, indeed, all thinking and action;
>
> b)   Be not only a statement of aims and
>   principles, but must also provide the
>   intellectual tools by which these aims
>   are achieved, and must concentrate on

all constructive thinking around
achieving those aims; and,

c) Offer the ordinary man and woman some
concrete, tangible and realizable hope of
better life   within his or her life-time.9

Nkrumaism thus presented, there began a full-
scale intellectual, educational and organizational
work to propagate it. The seminaries decided to
standardize Nkrumaism as a philosophy and also
suggested that it be taught officially in all
schools. The curricular planning was to take
place at the Ideological Institute. In addition
to Nkrumaism, the Institute also offered courses
in Political Science, Political Economy of
Socialism, nationalism, history, government,
philosophy, state enterprises, social welfare and
community development, scientific socialism,
constitutional law, and physical culture and
sports.

The objective of the Institute was:10

a)   To provide ideological education to
activists and Freedom Fighters of the
African struggle against imperialism,
colonialism and neo-colonialism.

b)   To provide socialist education bearing
on the projection of African
personality.

c)   To prepare seminars and forum
discussions as a means of providing
refresher courses for students and
nationalists as well as functionaries in
the African Liberation Movement.

There were no academic requirements for
admission. Admission was open to all students of
popular political parties of the various African
countries, trade unions, youth, women's and other
political organizations struggling for national
independence as well as for the unity of the
entire African continent. These students were
sponsored by the above organizations.

The syllabus for Nkrumaism was as follows:

1.   Arrival of Dr. Kwame Nkrumah, General
Secretary of U.G.C.C.

2.   Formation   of   the   C.Y.O.   within   the
U.G.C.C.

3.   Formation of the C.P.P.

4.   The   Demand   for   Universal   Adult
      Suffrage--Ghana People's Representative
      Assembly, 20th November 1949.

5.   The Struggle for Real Independence:

      a)   Positive Action

      b)   Tactical Action--the challenge.

6.   Constitutional Changes:

      a)   Internal Self-Government.

      b)   The   Defeat   of   the   National
      Bourgeoisie   and   Reactionary   Elite
      (G.C.P.,   N.L.M.,   U.P.)   in   the
      popular demand for unitary form   of
      Government--abolition   of   regional
      assemblies.

      c)   Full Independence.

7.   Economic Reconstruction.

8.   Party Organization and the Ideological
      Platforms of the Party:

      a)   General   Concept   of   Party
      Organization and   Discipline.

      b)   Ghana Trade Union Congress.

      c)   United Ghana Farmers' Council.

      d)   Cooperatives.

      e)   Workers Brigade.

      f)   Young Pioneers.

      g)   National Council of Ghana   Women.

9.   Philosophy   of   Nkrumaism--Its   General
      Principles:

      a)   The   application   of   scientific
      socialism for the development of Ghana

in particular and Africa as a whole. The history and tenets of the Convention People's Party based on a detailed study of the life and writings of Osagyefo Dr. Kwame Nkrumah.

b) The building of a socialist state and the basic principles as outlined in the speeches and articles of Osagyefo Dr. Kwame Nkrumah and other leaders of the Party.

c) The struggle for political and economic liberation from imperialism and the tasks in Ghana.

d) (i) The struggle for complete African unity as the foundation for the rapid political and economic liberation of all of Africa and for the well-being of its people.

(ii) Foreign Policy. e) Party Structure.

f) The leading role of the Convention People's Party and its organizational structure.

g) Cultural aspect of Nkrumaism.11

Except for the Director of the Institute, Kwadwo Addison, the tutorial staff was comprised of a highly competent group of scholars--J.M. Perczynski, Ph.D.; Paul Kovaly, Ph.D.; R. Annoh-Oprensem, M.A.; J. Kwasi Nsarkoh, L.L.D.; Tibor Szamuely, Ph.D.; S.G. Ikoku, M.Sc.; Bankole Akpata, Ph.D.; Boris Petruck, ph.D.; W.E. Abraham, B.A., B. Phill.; W.C. Ekow-Daniels, L.I.M., Ph.D.

Inaugurating the first course of ideological education in Ghana , Nkrumah, in his usual political rhetoric, said with a prophetic perspicacity:

When, therefore, I have come to this town of Winneba to lay the foundation stone of the Kwame Nkrumah Institute and to inaugurate the first course in ideological training....I see a beam of hope shooting across our continent, for the things which will be taught in this Institute will strengthen African youth and manhood and

inspire it to scale great heights; and the
men and women who will pass through this
Institute will go out not only armed with
analytical knowledge to wage the battle of
scientific socialism, but will also be
fortified with a keen spirit of education and
service to our Fatherland.12

Speaking before the National Assembly on
October 2, 1962, Nkrumah asserted that intervening
events have emphasized the soundness of Nkrumaism
as a political ideology and its moral purpose. He
called for vigilance on the part of party
activists and the masses "to build an African
state based on African ideals and upholding the
dignity and personality of the African so long
submerged by colonialism."

The editors of THE SPARK•13• have termed this
vigilance the ideology of positive action, which
they argue is socialism. In order to effectuate
this African state based on African ideals and the
dignity and personality of the African in an age
of progressive techno-cultural westernization of
the world, the Nkrumaist must set out consciously
to grapple with certain issues "if independence is
not to be alienated from the people." These
ideologically elevated issues are:

1)   To seek a connection with the
     egalitarian and humanist past of the
     people before their social evolution was
     ravaged by colonialism;

2)   To seek from colonialism those elements
     like new methods of industrial
     production and economic organization
     which can be adopted to serve the
     interests of the people;

3)   To seek ways and means of crushing the
     growth of class inequalities and
     antagonisms created by the capitalist
     habit of colonialism;

4)   To reclaim the psychology of the people
     by erasing "colonial mentality";

5)   To defend the independence and security
of the people.14

Based on the speeches, statements and
writings of Nkrumah, which form the foundations of

Nkrumaism as an ideology, we shall attempt in the
concluding part of this chapter an analytic
interpretation of the moral, social, psychological
and ethical aspects of Nkrumaism.

Another aspect of Nkrumaism deals with the
socialization process of the youth. Speaking
before the seminarians at the Ideological
Institute, he said:

> The youth must be imbued not only with a
> keen spirit of patriotism, but also with a
> sense of lofty socialist ideals which will
> enable them to think and act in the best
> interests of the community as a whole and not
> in the interest of themselves as
> individuals.15

To effectuate this, Nkrumah suggested this
approach:

> The Secretariat of the Bureau of Party
> Education must now go to the people; it must
> go to the ward, town and village branches as
> well as to the special branches created in
> the offices, shops, factories, state farms,
> corporations and other places of employment,
> carrying its work to our general membership.
> It must go to the primary schools through the
> Young Pioneers; it must go to the secondary
> schools; colleges and universities. And here
> it is proper that we confine Party Study
> Groups to secondary schools, colleges and
> universities. In this connection I suggest
> that Education Secretaries should be
> appointed wherever a Party branch is
> established, and these should undertake Party
> educational work in addition to their normal
> duties.16

Nkrumaism is not only concerned with ideological
education, but is also responsible for the
guidance of general education in such a way as to
satisfy the needs of the nation. It is a basic
principle of Nkrumaism to frame the educational
program of the country so as to preserve the
spiritual and cultural identity of the nation and
to guarantee to the youth of the nation the
development of personality and a unity of purpose.
Nkrumaism considers education not merely a method
of public instruction, but a process through which
a nation develops true self-consciousness. It
consists in the training of the new generation in

the arts and crafts of living and in making them
realize their mission and duty. Through
education, Nkrumaism argues, people communicate
their culture to the future generation and inspire
them with the ideals of life. It is a mental,
physical and moral training and its objective is
to produce dedicated men and good citizens. "We
lay stress on education because it is the antidote
to feudalist despotism and ignorance and
superstition."17 Speaking at Adisadel College on
November 10, 1955, Nkrumah stated inter alia:

> The purpose of all true education is to
> produce good citizens...particularly ...those
> principles of good citizenship which will
> help him (the student) to take a full share
> of the work of the community when he leaves
> school. He learns to shoulder
> responsibilities, to share with his fellows
> both the good and bad things of life, to
> understand the importance of team spirit and
> to take a personal pride in the success of
> the...community. And, perhaps more important
> still is the fact that he learns to live in
> tolerance and cooperation with his fellow
> student.•18

This is the importance of education, argues
Nkrumaism. Responsible governments the world over
have always recognized this basic fact. A
scrupulous study of history reveals that this
importance increases when some especially
important political or economic revolution occurs.
Most important, such revolutions have been
followed by radical change in education and its
ideals, methods, and plans. The industrial
revolution was followed by the new public
education policy in England. American education
underwent a basic change and became democratic and
national after the Civil War. After the Russian
Revolution, a basic change in education occurred--
education was universalized. History is replete
with such examples.

And in his concluding remarks at Adisadel
College, Nkrumah said to the students:

> Set yourselves up as an example and
> prove to the world that you are both capable
> and ready to put your country on the map, to
> hoist her flag and to keep it flying. Above
> all, don't become know-alls, for nothing
> makes one look more of a fool. Education

makes us humble and tolerant. You can do
well to remember these lines of William
Cowper:

"Knowledge is proud that he had learned
so much; wisdom is humble that he knows no
more."19

Another aspect of Nkrumaism deals with the
family as the corner-stone of social structure.
The marital bond, according to Nkrumaism, is
perhaps the one most important social act in
society. Thus, Nkrumaism rejects polygamous
marriage and considers it a threat to the very
fabric of family life and society. With a view to
safeguarding the family structure and maintaining
a healthy home atmosphere in which the young would
receive adequate training, in an atmosphere of
complete equality between the sexes, Nkrumaism
declared the polygamous marriage inappropriate but
recognized the reality of polygamy in Ghana. The
C.P.P. in presenting its Program for Work and
Happiness•20 took a strong position on marriage.
The Program stated, inter alia:

Our marriage laws are at present a
mixture of our own indigenous forms and the
system existing in the advanced
industrialized nations which we inherited
through colonialism. The new circumstances
which have been created by a changing socio-
economic pattern and the popularization of
education with its increasing movement of
people from village to town and subsequent
break-up of clan-life, makes the polygamous
systems of marriage inappropriate. New forms
of family life are breaking up the old
loyalties. Moreover, the Party stands for
complete equality between the sexes and
complete equality is, strictly speaking,
incompatible with polygamy.

The Party believes that there should be
only one form of marriage, and that is
monogamy. It recognizes, however, that
existing polygamous marriages will not
disappear with the enforcement by law of
monogamy. Hence there can be no legal or
social discrimination against children in the
form of illegitimacy, which is completely
alien to our African custom. The State's
responsibility in the new social order will

be to all children and not merely those from
monogamous marriages.

Another aspect of Nkrumaism deals with the
principle of social cohesion which is, perhaps the
one most important principle of Nkrumaism. This
principle can be described as follows: (a)
Nkrumaism starts with the relationship between the
individual and his own conscience. The individual
is duty-bound to avail himself of the good things
of life, to give himself a fair share of work and
rest so that he may not succumb to exhaustion from
overwork. The self-training of the individual in
this manner is but a preparation for the role
which he is called upon to play in the new social
order. (b) Nkrumaism then moves from the realm
of the individual to that of the family. The
family structure, according to Nkrumaism, is based
on the interdependence of advantages and
liabilities, rights and obligations. Such
cohesion is not confined to economic affairs
alone, it is all-embracing in its scope and
includes the financial maintenance of the family,
the protection of marital relations and of
motherhood,21 the obligation of caring for the
children physically, mentally, and spiritually,
and the duty of the children towards their parents
in old age. To the extent that the individual
members of the family care for and protect one
another, the social obligations of the state are
reduced and lightened. (c) Proceeding from the
realm of the family to the wider social structure,
one finds the principle of social cohesion as an
indispensable element in all social relationships
not merely in the sphere of economics, but also in
that of ethics. Every individual, according to
Nkrumaism, is duty-bound to perform his own job to
the best of his ability because the fruits of his
labor necessarily affect the society as a whole.
He is obliged, therefore, to refrain from evil
deeds and to endeavor to persuade others to follow
his example.22 (d) In the sphere of economics,
Nkrumaism does not treat economic science
independently of moral considerations. Man's life
is regarded by Nkrumaism as an entity composed of
material and moral elements. Whenever ethical
demands are not supported by positive injunctions
relating to a positive material life, a gap
between ethics and reality becomes inevitable.
(e) In the sphere of transnational politics,
Nkrumaism hopes to see an Ibn-Batuta of today
travels from the West Coast of Africa to the Coast
of the Indian Ocean and nowhere would be be an

alien and everywhere there would be chances for him to become a judge, a minister, or an ambassador.23

Another ingredient of Nkrumaism is Pan-Africanism. The C.P.P. in its "Programme on Work and Happiness" put forth the following:

1. Nkrumaism teaches that in Africa today it is totally impossible to make a division between internal policy and foreign policy. For national prosperity and national progress within individual African States at the present stage of historical development depend largely upon the extent of cooperation between all the States. As long as Africa remains balkanized, no single State upon our continent can be really prosperous. Once Africa is united, no single African State can fail to share in the increased prosperity that union will bring.

2. Nkrumaism teaches that small States are even more vulnerable than the Great Powers to destruction in a global war, and, therefore, all countries, the small no less than the great must do all they can to secure world peace. This cannot be done by means of passive neutralism. It has to be achieved through a positive policy of non-alignment, which will provide a bridge between the world's two great rival powers.

3. Nkrumaism, which is based on scientific socialism, is all-pervading, and while its theory in full can only be developed in and around the Party leadership, it must influence in some form all education and indeed all thinking and action. Nkrumaism must be not only a statement of aims and principles. It must also provide the intellectual tools by which these aims are achieved and must concentrate on all constructive thinking around achieving these aims. Nkrumaism must also offer the ordinary man and woman some concrete, tangible and realizable hope of a better life within his or her lifetime. Nkrumaism poses a full scale intellectual, educational and organizational attack on

colonialism and neo-colonialism, in all
their forms and manifestations.

4.   Nkrumaism teaches further that non-
      alignment is a positive policy because
      it allows the country following it to
      maintain its sovereignty by taking a
      definite and independent stand on
      international issues. This has a very
      salutary effect on reducing world
      tension and promoting peace by
      establishing a firm balance between the
      two power blocs.24

Issuing from the above tenets, socialist
planning, socialist vigilance, morality and
dynamism, argues Nkrumah, can only spring from a
sound socialist ideology, i.e. Nkrumaism.25
Therefore, all Ministers in the Cabinet were
required to attend a course of ideological study
and self-examination because "our socialist
ideology contains the great truths and realities
of our age.26 The intent of this self-examination
was to rid the Ministers and Party functionaries
of the "desperate rush to 'get rich quick'".27
Faced with this problem of the abuse of power
through dishonesty by some of his Ministers and
Party functionaries, Nkrumah sounded this warning:

         The abuse of power through dishonesty is
      an abomination. The misuse of office for
      selfish ends is a crime against the Party and
      the State, and therefore a greater
      abomination. The Convention People's Party
      is the servant of the people, and therefore
      the men whom it puts into office and power
      must use that opportunity to serve the
      people, remembering at all times that
      selfless and loyal service is a reward in
      itself.28

Nkrumaism must not be taken as meaning
"African Socialism". Nkrumah argued that "African
Socialism" is meaningless and irrelevant to the
"realities of the diverse and irreconcilable
social, political, and economic policies being
pursued by African States today", and he rejects
the view that "traditional African Society was a
classless society imbued with the spirit of
humanism." He argues that such a conception of
socialism "makes a fetish of the communal African
society," and that the realities of African
society "were somewhat more sordid."29

"All available evidence from the history of Africa, up to the eve of the European colonization," Nkrumah argues, "shows that African society was neither classless nor devoid of a social hierarchy. Feudalism existed in some parts of Africa before colonization; and feudalism involves a deep and exploitive social stratification, founded on the ownership of Land. It must also be noted that slavery existed in Africa before European colonization, although the earlier European contact gave slavery in Africa some of its most vicious characteristics. The truth remains, however, that before colonization, which became widespread in Africa only in the nineteenth century, Africans were prepared to sell, often for no more than thirty pieces of silver, fellow tribesmen and even members of the same 'extended' family and clan. Colonialism deserves to be blamed for many evils in Africa, but surely it was not preceded by an African Golden Age or paradise. A return to the precolonial African society is evidently not worthy of the ingenuity and efforts of our people."30

What Nkrumah, therefore, proposes is that what socialist thought in Africa must recapture "is not the structure of the 'traditional African Society' but its spirit, for the spirit of communalism is crystallized in its humanism and in its reconciliation of the individual advancement with group welfare."31 Therefore in bringing about a new social order (see Chapters V and VI) in a traditional African society, Nkrumah categorically states that "We postulate each man to be an end in himself, not merely a means; and we accept the necessity of guaranteeing each man equal opportunities for his development. The implications of this for socio-political practice have to be worked out scientifically, and the necessary social and economic policies pursued with resolution. Any meaningful humanism must begin from egalitarianism and must lead to objectively chosen policies for safeguarding and sustaining egalitarianism.32

This approach to safeguarding and sustaining egalitarianism, Nkrumah argues, requires an ideology--not a return to the communalistic society of ancient Africa--an ideology which is a synthesis of Islamic civilization, and European colonialism which have "permanently changed the complexion of the traditional African society."33

Starting from this premise, Nkrumah sees modern
African societies as not being traditional; they
are only "in a state of socio-economic
disequilibrium. They are in this state because
they are not anchored to a steadying ideology."34
Thus the need for a national ideology not only as
a political tool, but as a factor for national
unity.

To move to the second phase of the
revolution, the economic and social reconstruction
of Ghana, Nkrumah had to consolidate his powers
and leadership and that of the Convention People's
Party as the only legitimate political party in
Ghana. In the next chapter we shall examine how
Nkrumah maximized his powers and that of the
C.P.P. We shall also attempt to examine the
techniques and approaches used by Nkrumah in
maximizing his political power and elevating
himself to the pivotal position he occupied in
Ghanaian society until the military coup of 1966.

REFERENCES

1.   Kwame Nkrumah, CONSCIENCISM, Heineman,
      London, 1964, p. 70.

2.   Ibid., p. 79.

3.   Speech by Nkrumah to the National
      Assembly on October 2, 1962.

4.   Ibid.

5.   Nkrumah, CONSCIENCISM, p. 68.

6.   Ibid.

7.   Ibid., pp. 56-57.

8.   Nkrumah, GUIDE TO PARTY ACTION (Accra,
      Ghana, February 3, 1962), p. 3.

9.   Ibid.

10.   "Prospectus" of Kwame Nkrumah
      Ideological Institute (Winneba, Ghana),
      p. 5.

11.   Ibid., pp. 12-13.

12. Speech by Kwame Nkrumah at the laying of the foundation stone of the Institute at Winneba on February 18, 1961.

13. Editors of THE SPARK, SOME ESSENTIAL FEATURES OF NKRUMAISM (International Publishers, New York, 1965), pp. 122-123.

14. Ibid.

15. Nkrumah, GUIDE TO PARTY ACTION, p. 6.

16. Ibid., p. 5.

17. Kwame Nkrumah, I SPEAK OF FREEDOM (New York, 1961), p. 45.

18. Ibid., pp. 57-58.

19. Ibid., p. 59.

20. PROGRAMME OF THE CONVENTION PEOPLE'S PARTY FOR WORK AND HAPPINESS (1961), pp. 34-35.

21. Ibid., p. 35.

22. Nkrumah, GUIDE TO PARTY ACTION, pp. 8-13.

23. See Kwame Nkrumah, AFRICA MUST UNITE (1963) for an exposition of this view.

24. PROGRAMME FOR WORK AND HAPPINESS, pp. 6-7.

25. Nkrumah, BLUEPRINT FOR THE FUTURE (August 24, 1965), p. 9.

26. Ibid.

27. Ibid., p. 10.

28. Nkrumah, GUIDE TO PARTY ACTION, pp. 9-10.

29. Kwame Nkrumah, "African Socialism Revisited," AFRICAN FORUM, Vol. I, No. 3, Winter 1966, pp. 4-5.

30. Ibid., p. 5.

31.   Ibid.

32.   Ibid., p. 6.

33.   Ibid., p. 7.

34.   Ibid.

MAXIMIZATION CF POLITICAL POWER

In the preceding chapter we have deliberately
refrained frcm referring to Nkrumah as a
charismatic leader, though he had a period of
charismatic leadership when he attracted large
crowds, was hoisted on the shoulders of party
activists and celebrated in "hi-life" songs.   If
we accept Karl Loewenstein's observation1 that Max
Weber's idea of charisma derives from the
religious realm and that Weber undertook to
transfer it to the realm of politics, we must
assert that the world of religion proper remains
the fundamental locus of charismatic leadership.
Nkrumah's period cf charismatic leadership,
however, was a period characterized by overt signs
of popularity and spontaneous affection and
devotion, which led to an acceptance of him as a
national hero. But to be a charismatic leader, it
is essential to possess extraordinary qualities.
The crucial test of charisma, as Weber stresses,
is the response cf the followers: "It is the
recognition cn the part of those subject to
authority which is decisive for the validity of
charisma."2   This recognition is not alone
sufficiently a claim to charismatic leadership.
The leader must show "signs" cr "proof" of his
extraordinary qualities and demonstrate
exceptional abilities if his followers are to
continue to render him their personal devotion.
Should he fail to demonstrate his charismatic
powers over an extended period of time, his
charismatic authority may wither away. As Weber
asserts:

> By its very nature, the existence of
> charismatic authority is specifically
> unstable. The holder may forego his
> charisma; he may feel "forsaken by his God",
> as Jesus did on the cross; he may prove to
> his followers that "virtue is gone out of
> him". It is then that his mission is
> extinguished, and hope waits and searches for
> a new holder of charisma.3

Charismatic leadership with all its religious connotation applies chiefly to the pre-Cartesian West and, in modern times, to the third world which has not yet extricated itself from the "magico-religious ambiance."4

Before analyzing Nkrumah's attempt to maximize his political power in Ghana, let us first indicate some of the problems faced by Nkrumah and the convention People's Party.

How do leaders in transitional societies maintain themselves in the seat of authority and wield power? Bearing in mind that the political systems of these societies are constantly in flux, and that they are greatly influenced by internal and external factors, it behooves us first to identify the transhistorical variables in the modernization process in these societies: (1) The organization of society along a concept totally new--the modern state; (2) The differentiation of a distinct political function; (3) The creation of a modern public service; (4) The involvement in the political process of groups which in the past did not participate in it; and (5) The evolution of public policy to cope with the forces of social change set in motion by the modernist impact.5

In like manner, Nkrumah and the leadership of the C.P.P. constantly may have asked themselves these transhistorical questions: (1) Do we have sufficient power to survive beyond a given date? (2) Do we have sufficient power to accomplish our social and political objectives? (3) Whom can we count upon for support for our policies? (4) Do we have the tools to manipulate the behavior of the newly emancipated and participant masses? (5) How do we extend our bases of support? (6) Who are our opponents? (7) How do we ensure that we would not be overtaken by events and be overthrown by our opponents? (8) What politically relevant groups are rising in influence to challenge us and which ones are declining? (9) Which of these changes are the result of leadership factors, improved or faltering skill at political organization? (10) What are the grounds for the development of major protest movements? (11) What is the mix or balance between agitational skills and real socio-economic issues in the strength of opposition and protest movements? (12) How large a proportion of the population participates in the present political process of our country? To what extent? (13) Is there a sharp urban-rural

division? How is this changing and at what rate?
Under the impact of what forces? (14) Has our
ideology been accepted or is there a competing
ideology within our country which will eventually
challenge us? If there is a competing ideology,
what, then, are our strengths and weaknesses as
political leaders?

These are some of the vexatious questions
faced by Nkrumah and the C.P.P. They were
concrete and central to the concerns of Nkrumah
and the C.P.P.

These questions were posed with critical
urgency in Ghana between 1960-65. We shall show
later on how Nkrumah faced some of these
questions. At the risk of overstating the
obvious, let us mention in passing that those who
inherited the "colonial legacy" on March 6, 1957,
with the possible exception of a few, actually
never participated in the formal governmental
administration of the Gold Coast. Therefore, they
did not profit from any long established
institutionalized framework of values. By 1957,
when Ghana was declared independent, there were no
rules restraining them from extremism except Party
rules. They became preoccupied with the problems
of power and implementing their party's programs.

Given the nature of the political system (it
was in a state of uncertainty), Nkrumah became
preoccupied with the maximization of political
power, essentially because his aspirations for
modernity were being obstructed by the Right
Opposition and the traditional elites. In order
to effect his party's PROGRAM FOR WORK AND
HAPPINESS and to establish a viable political
system in which the legitimacy of the government
and the Presidency as a national office would be
universally accepted, and with the C.P.P. serving
as the vehicle of resolving all socio-political
conflicts, Nkrumah finally decided to make Ghana a
one-party state.

In the newness of his political leadership,
Nkrumah shared many similar political and economic
problems with leaders of other transitional
societies. The crux in understanding the
maximization of political power in Ghana between
1960-65 is the schism between Nkrumah on the one
hand, and the Right Opposition and traditional
elites on the other, i.e. the difference between
leadership and authority. As Professor Bierstedt
puts it in the sociological sense:

A leader can only request, an authority can require....Leadership depends upon the personal qualities of the leader in the situation in which he leads. In the case of authority, however, the relationship ceases to be personal and, if the legitimacy of the authority is recognized, the subordinate must obey the command even when he is unacquainted with the person who issues it. In a leadership relation, the person is basic; in an authority relation the person is merely a symbol.6

A basic problem Nkrumah faced was the welding of disparate tribal groups who had traditionally given their allegiance to the traditional authority--the chief--into a unified political community--Ghana. In a newly independent, tribalized and changing society, political consensus was problematic, because Ghana is basically a traditional society composed of many tribes, languages and backgrounds. Ghana is a society which is as yet partially integrated, socially,

Ghana of the colonial era was a society with many models and styles. New heroes and old ones coexisted side by side--the traditional leaders and the school teachers, the lawyers and the businessmen, the classical scholars and the urban protonationalist activists. On the eve of independence, March 6, 1957, the urban protonationalist activists dominated the political scene and Nkrumah emerged as a giant among political and intellectual pygmies.

The success of Nkrumah in maximizing his political power was due partly to his effective use of the techniques of manipulative behavior and partly to the methods of elite recruitment. These techniques and methods which he introduced touched off a complex process of political socialization and changed the effectiveness and performance of the Right Opposition and the traditional elites. Professor Almond theoretically points out that:

In political systems, the emergence of mass parties or mass media of communication changes the performance of all the other structures of the political system, and affects the general capabilities of the system in its domestic...environment. In other words, when one variable in a system changes in magnitude or in quality, the others are subjected to strains and are transformed, and the system changes its pattern of performance.7

Between 1960 and 1965, Ghana was a highly politicized society. Fragile national integration and economic and socio-cultural mobility was compensated for by political control; and the political authority of the C.P.P. was officially legitimated as a result of the ineffectiveness of the Right Opposition.

Ghana was highly politicized not because Ghanaians are inherently interested in politics, but because the scope of political decisions was wide and things that mattered were politically linked. Moreover, the effects of the political authority of Nkrumah and the C.P.P. were sharply visible and were immediately consequential. The line between the political and the non-political was trivial.

The struggle for political power during this period was very intense. Nkrumah attempted to maximize political power by associating with himself others who had the ability to influence the behavior of the newly emancipated masses.

In this, Nkrumah utilized the extra-legal influence he had acquired in rewarding the activists of the C.P.P. who could influence the emancipated masses by inducing changes in the political system which benefited his supporters and prevented those changes which his supporters feared the most, i.e., recruitment of new elites into the C.P.P. And, in this process of maximizing political power, Nkrumah's force of personality replaced the functions and authority of the traditional elites. Professor Apter has identified four types of structures of Nkrumah's personality which replaced the function and authority of these traditional elites:

1. SANCTIONAL SOURCE - Whereas the experience of sanction stemmed from the chief acting as trustee for the ancestors, Nkrumah became a sanctional source in and of himself. He became a source of norms which, having been made explicit, became a standard for his followers.

2. SYMBOLIC REFERRENT - Where the chief was the central orientaticnal symbol of local tribal unity continuity, and integration, through which members of the system related in social and political intercourse, Nkrumah became the symbolic referrent in which widely differing sccial groups find orientational identity with cne another.

3. INTEGRATICNAL INTEGER - Where the chief was the central figure in the pattern of traditional authority through which legitimized power was expressed in institutionalized role structures within hierarchical patterns, Nkrumah became an independent central figure, expressing charismatic authcrity fcr groups in the system within a dependent party structure, integrated within a legal framework of British governmental units.

4. SUB-ETHNIC OR ETHNIC DEFINITION - Where the Chief was the central figure expressing membership and group-interrelation based upon blccd, clan and lineage in traditicnal society, Nkrumah became the symbcl of Ghana and African membership based upon nativity and racial definiticn transcending localized cultural limits to a more generalized African "Ghana" definition.8

The struggle for the attempted maximization of political power during these five years was, indeed, not an easy one. The political stakes were very great. There was no expanding economy or opportunity for careers opened to talent, other than the political field, and it was easy for an eminent politician, civil servant, or businessman to find himself catapulted into an cblivicn from which he might never extricate himself. After all, where can former Ministers, Ambassadors, and Generals find jobs with dignity in a society in which everything is politically ccntrclled? There are not enough university chancellorships or corporaticn presidencies available.

Maximizing political power to perform the necessary governmental functions is nct an end in itself. It is only a means by which the party in power at any given mcment has its way in the pclitical process to advance that continuity of policy and political stability which sooner or later must underlay the effectuaticn of a new political order replacing the colonial legacy.

By examining this process cf attempted maximization cf political power, we are by no means suggesting that those who maximize political power should carry it to the extreme because of the relative instability of their regimes, as was the case with Nkrumah. Butm one can argue for a substantial degree of political power to be concentrated in the hands of those with executive authority and responsibility in transitional societies. The sui generis character of transiticnal sccieties is that they all suffer not so much frcm an overabundance of maximized political power, but rather from an insufficiency of a respcnsibly maximized political pcwer.

Indeed, the very attempt at rationalization, by leaders of transiticnal societies, of the centralizing and coercive tendencies of their regimes, must be viewed with suspicion because the ccuntries are newly independent, insufficiently develofed politically, eccnomically, and socially, and have a relatively small number of trained administrators. As Professor Martin Kilson points out, "centralization in the form of the single-party regime, with a top-heavy bureaucracy handling tasks better left to cthers, is simply beside the fcint. That is, it is beside the point of what is needed for sound develcpment, but very much to the pcint of the insatiable appetite of politicians for power and ill-gained wealth."9

With these observations serving as a background, we will prcceed to discuss our method of affroach in analyzing the strategies employed by Nkrumah in his attempts to maximize his political power, i.e., the acquisiticn of the highest possible degree of political pcwer.

In the absence of any scholarly work dealing with Nkrumah's method of attempting to maximize his fclitical power, our categorical generalizaticns regarding his method may not be the final view. Nevertheless, it will be interesting, tc say the least, to ccnstruct from the assemblage of events and processes a coherent picture of this method. In doing so we will investigate the fundamental causes, and then seek tc interpret the results by making clear the relaticnships which they have to each cther and to the method as a whole. We will alsc attempt to indicate the characteristics of a given stage in the process and the analytical relations to preceding stages in the process which make the succeeding stages possible. And, finally, we will indicate the universe for which the generality of common and distinctive variables is possible. Though we start with an investigation of the fundamental causes, we must admit that we do not possess a perfect and complete knowledge of all the minor relations and proximate causes.

1. BASIC APPROACHES TO MAXIMIZING POLITICAL POWER

So far, we have mainly focused on Nkrumah because he was a figure omnipresent in the Ghanaian political process, and as the maker of policy, originator and recipient of messages, performer of functions, wielder of political power, and originator and operator of institutions; he brought these disparate elements into a single, visible focus. Our focus has been on Nkrumah's leadership, because leadership itself is an instrument of change. But as we shall see in the following analysis, Nkrumah's exercise of political power was strikingly different from the methods which he advocated.

As to Nkrumah's basic approach to maximizing political power between 1960 and 1965, a careful analysis of the Ghanaian political process reveals the following techniques:

a. APPROACH A: THE PROBLEM SOLVING METHOD. Nkrumah was dedicated to the proposition that his political survival would best be insured by an orderly, systematic and sustained effort at solving periodic crises besetting the political system, i.e., economic problems, harmonious integration of the various tribes, the problem of absorbing the new elites into the political system, and the problem of replacing traditional authority with regular civil authority.

This approach required Nkrumah to depend on a top-heavy bureaucracy, the leadership of the Trades Union Congress, and the Ghana Farmers' Council-leaderships with the required competence and energy to withstand the designated problems. This approach subsumes that a political leader has time to carry out his programs and that as specific problems are grappled with some degree of administrative efficiency and political effectiveness, thereby minimizing tension in the political system.

It is a method which requires the availability of political patronage, such as important governmental posts for the political activists and the loyal followers to undercut the effectiveness of the criticism of the opposition, i.e., the Right Opposition and the traditional elites, and the restlessness of the masses. It also requires a consensus between the political leader and the other elements in the society on whom he depends for support of his programs, as to what problems are urgent and worth grappling with. If the political leader is shrewd enough, he defines the problems, and puts his propaganda machinery to work to engineer a consensus, or he may just employ coercive techniques to force the desired consensus.

This approach provided a sense of expanding opportunities to the restless masses. The degree of effectiveness with which Nkrumah succeeded in grappling with certain crises, e.g. the 1960 general strike of the Railway and Harbor Workers' Union, and the threat of the T.U.C. to launch a "political strike" when their leader was removed from office and made the National organizer of the Ghana Builders' Brigade in 1960, enhanced Nkrumah's self-confidence and effectiveness as a political leader. And, furthermore, the degree of political participation which Nkrumah allowed the newly emancipated masses, negated the effectiveness of his opponents. Nkrumah gave the masses a degree of satisfaction by enabling them to be politically active, an opportunity which the opposition denied them.

But this approach had its weakness, as the overthrow of Nkrumah clearly demonstrated. "Leaders pursuing this strategy are not likely to cut much of a figure. Charisma will be inconspicuous. Warmth will be missing. The risk of such a strategy is popular boredom. There is not much excitement to it. Particularly after the excitement of the independence 'struggles' public life will have lost an important...perhaps a critical...quality of savor."10

b. APPROACH B: THE PSYCHOLOGICAL METHOD. This method was a response to the fact that political participation in Ghana was (and still is) highly emotional. Not only in Ghana, but in many other transitional societies, "large

numbers of articulate people experience a high
level of anxiety. Old patterns are breaking down
and new ones have not yet been found. There is a
crisis of identity, as men seek that sense of
uniqueness and of possessing special qualities out
of which alone self-respect can come. Sometimes
societies are so fraught with fissures that only
intense and overriding feelings will permit men to
identify with others in that same society,
transcending traditional and tribal differences in
shared emotions which alone can weaken primordial,
traditional attachments."11

Nkrumah, more than any other Ghanaian
politician, realized this phenomenon early in the
struggle for independence, and from 1960 to 1965
used this psychological factor to maintain himself
in power. While using the psychological method of
times he relegated the governmental structure to
the background and aroused the masses by appealing
to their emotions. This approach to maximizing
power "has the virtue of touching the deeper
springs of man's motivation". It led "to a
revolutionary infusion of national solidarity and
identification." It promoted "collaboration by
dramatizing a shared purpose, the more easily
agreed to because it was pitched at a high
emotional level."12

This approach needed enemies and scapegoats
for some of the problems which Nkrumah was not
able to solve, i.e., essentially economic
problems. Nkrumah, therefore, dramatized the
dangers from foreign economic interests,
particularly of the West. This led to an
indictment of the West.13 Failing to cope with
the economic problems, he used elements of a
foreign presence, i.e., the Peace Corps, Agency
for International Development, the World Bank, as
useful targets for induced mass hostility.

The political genius of Nkrumah lies in the
fact that he almost immediately realized that
sooner or later his convenient enemies and
scapegoats might be gone and that if he were to
project Ghana as a unified nation-state without
its tribal diversity, he must project a Pan-
African image and attempt to unify hitherto
colonial appendages, or undertake some form of
verbal attack against a neighboring country.
Though many have found this strategy wanting, it
did cope with some real problems and promoted not
only Nkrumah's domestic position as a leader, but

it helped project Nkrumah as an African leader. He succeeded in sustaining the intensity of excitement by drawing large numbers of individuals into constant political agitation--an activity which provided "many immediate psychic rewards to the people actively mobilized for this purpose."

The psychological method, however, is fraught with weaknesses and dangers. As Wriggins points out, "keeping the pitch of excitement is difficult. Economic problems tend to mount and lead to growing frustrations. The more sophisticated are unlikely to be caught up in the popular excitement and increasingly consider this strategy ill-advised and become progressively less enthusiastic. The excitement may lead to unpredictability, a growing sense of insecurity and whim. It may open the way to the organizational activities of extremists. It may call for progressive intimidation."14 It was precisely the intimidation of individuals that Nkrumah adopted as his last technique in maximizing political power.

c. APPROACH C: INTIMIDATION. Since in Ghana political traditions were ill-defined, it was easy for Nkrumah to intimidate individuals of all social strata. In a country that was beset with traditional and tribal recriminations, a country that has had no history of political freedom, it was relatively easy for Nkrumah to induce silence and "sufficient" obedience from the masses. Political opposition was silenced, and the press and all other associational and non-associational organizations were induced to toe the party's line. A systematic effort to identify possible opponents of the political system and to induce them to be silent or go abroad was vigorously pursued by Nkrumah. This led to the creation of obscure ambassadorial posts. In the last analysis, there was always the mysterious disappearance of an opponent or his political incarceration without trial.

The Convention People's Party was the vehicle through which Nkrumah informed himself of what was going on in Ghana. It was the C.P.P. which he used to intimidate and to infuse into the civil servants, the army and police, businessmen, religious leaders, and the seats of higher learning the appropriate attitudes and performance which the intended political system demanded.

A serious by-product of this approach, as
Wriggins points out, "is the advantage this gives
to oppositionists trained in clandestine
organization. Beneath the surface of
intimidation, it is only the secretive,
conspirational parties which know how to
organize."15

The major problem Nkrumah faced was how to
sustain the other functions of government,
including solving grave economic problems, a
minimum degree of reliability and social and
political stability, and a sufficient degree of
consensus among the populace to permit the
political system to function while maintaining
mutual suspicion and intimidation at a high
level... Nkrumah attempted to solve this problem
through the strategy of political recruitment. If
political recruitment can be considered as an
indicator of the political system, and a central
function indicating the values of the system, we
must now turn our attention to the problem of
political recruitment.

2. POLITICAL RECRUITMENT

The elite recruitment pattern which Nkrumah
followed, both reflected and affected Ghanaian
society. As a factor which affected change or as
an independent variable, political recruitment
between 1960 and 1965 determined the avenues for
socialization of politicians and status,
influenced the policies that were enacted by the
government, retarded changes, effected the uneven
distribution of status and prestige, and finally
determined the degree of stability of the
political system. But more important, the elite
recruitment called for a ruthless manipulation of
the inevitable schism between different groups
within the system. What facilitated this
manipulation was the fact that at the beginning of
1960 there was consensus among the various groups,
i.e., the auxiliary branches of the C.P.P. on the
decision-making process, i.e., the Central
Committee of the C.P.P. This consensus was
instrumental in helping Nkrumah sustain himself in
power from 1960 to 1965, a period that may be
considered the most politically sensitive in the
post-independence era. As Professor Aron has
aptly stated: "The composition of the governing
elite may be progressively altered, the relative
importance of the various groups in the elite may
be changed, but a society can only survive and

prosper if there is true collaboration between
these groups. In one way or another there must be
unity of opinion and action on essential points in
the elite."16

In general, the political elites were
recruited from the ranks of the civil servants;
the urban-semi-educated class; the rural middle
and lower class; the cultural and traditionalist
groups; and the protonationalist activists.

The result of Nkrumah's method of political
recruitment was illuminated in the several changes
in the polity. It reflected economic changes in
the shifts from pre-industrial agricultural
emphasis to industry and from rural parochialism
to urban concentration; shifts in the political
infrastructure--the Party, the auxiliary
organizations of the party, the associational and
non-associational groups, the anomic groups--and
raised the level of political socialization and
the degree of political participation of the
masses. But although they were recruited for a
purpose transcending traditional and tribal
boundaries, they remained traditional and tribal
in background. They were only "emancipated
children of the traditional social structure".
While they accepted the new socio-political order
for which they were recruited, they were unable to
reject the old order of traditionalism and
tribalism.

This dualism between the new socio-political
order and the old traditionalistic tribalized
society forced Nkrumah to change his technique of
grappling with the problems of order and
stability. Political recruitment of elites of
various tribes into the C.P.P. and the government
had failed to forestall the struggle for tribal
representation and regionalism. This failure led
Nkrumah to believe that the struggle for tribal
representation and regionalism could destroy civil
order and stability in Ghana. The problems of
civil order and stability were overdue for
practical solution in Ghana, and in Nkrumah this
task found a politician who was equal to it.

The solution to the problem was found in the
introduction of a one-party system, and to be
sure, this solution was vigorously pursued at the
price of a systemic dysensus. But, Nkrumah
brought a new dimension and an understanding to
these problems.

Nkrumah attempted to solve this problem by declaring Ghana a one-party state in 1960, and proclaimed that there was no other authority except the authority of the state; no other ideology except the ideology of the C.P.P., the "vanguard of the people", and that any other ideology conducive to tribalism and regionalism was alien and thereby seditious.

One might be tempted to suggest that he searched for the solution to this problem and found it in the Hobbesian theory of representation. In resolving this sociological problem of order and stability, Hobbes opined:

> There is conscious to man a dictate of reason which disposes him to peace and obedience under civil order. Reason makes him, first, understand that he can live out his natural life in pursuit of his worldly happiness only under the condition that he lives in peace with his fellow-men; and it makes him, second, understand that he can live in peace, without distrust of the other man's intentions, only under the condition that every man's passions are curbed to mutual for-bearance by the overwhelming force of civil government.17

Under Nkrumah, civil authority and political stability met in the articulation of the political system into an ordered and stabilized existence. By an admixture of civil authority and political stability, the electorate was supposed to have actualized their orderly and peaceful existence.

Another evidence of Nkrumah's failure was that had it been different, Ghana could well have become a country with a socialist orientation. But the doctrinal and ideological interpretations advanced by Nkrumah through The Spark (the ideological journal of the C.P.P.) led to an absolutist kind of a political system. Hence, there was no freedom of debate over public issues; public expression of opinion and doctrine was suppressed; the C.P.P. and its intelligence unit had to decide who was to be allowed to speak in public, on what subject and in what manner; and there was censorship of the press and books. But there was freedom for those who propagated the ideology of the C.P.P.

3. STAGES OF POWER MAXIMIZATION

If politics as a consequence of socialization is a cognitive phenomenon that envelops people because of its universal nature, then research on transitional societies must be focused on the political elites as well as the historical experience of the people from a point of view of psychodynamic factors, in throwing light on the nature of a given political elite in a given transitional society at a given historical period.18 There are, however, difficulties to be encountered in this kind of research.19

What we are opining here is that by following this method of approach, we may be able to identify the types of ego-ideals chosen by these political leaders in their pre-adult lives as models for their later political careers, motivating them in directions congruent with their heroes' ideals; e.g., Nkrumah has called himself a Jeffersonian democrat, a non-denominational Marxist Christian, as well as an admirer of Ghandi. This problem of pre-adult experience has been dealt with by studies in political socialization.20

We must, however, point out that our mode of analysis does not presume to be of universal applicability. Our schema is that of studying a single case--the political style of Nkrumah. We must admit in passing that "the life of an individual cannot be adequately understood without references to the institutions within which his biography is enacted. For this biography records the acquiring, dropping, modifying, and in a very intimate way, the moving from one role to another...To understand the biography of an individual, we must understand the significance and meaning of the roles he has played and does play; to understand these roles we must understand the institutions of which they are a part."21

INTERPERSONAL STAGES OF POWER AGGREGATION

It is our contention that Nkrumah's approach to maximizing political power in general can be meaningfully described in terms of four successive stages of interpersonal relationships. Each stage or level was defined by a crucial interpersonal problem which was either solved or bypassed before he embarked on the next stage.

STAGE 1 - 1960: At Stage 1, the discrimination of differences between party members and non-members occurred.

(a) CCGNITION: Nkrumah, starting a new
political life in 1960 (cne-party system) with
very great awareness of the degree of diversity in
Ghana, certainly did not see himself as separate
frcm his political cpponents, since it was some
time before he even began to differentiate between
party members and the ideologically criented party
activists.22 Since he could not reduce political
tension without interacting with his political
opponents, he made some differentiaticn between
the party activists and the general public. At
first this was a gross political differentiation,
and both activists and card carrying members were
treated as relievers of basic tensions in the
political system.   For example, Nkrumah at this
stage of development made little of a
differentiaticn between the C.P.P. and his
political opponents. In addition, the range of
prcblems perceived was narrow, and barriers of
ideological differences wore thin.   As he later
began to perceive the fact that there was a strong
opposition to his ideological cpposition, he
realized that he was faced with the necessity of
reaching a ccmpromise with the cpposition or of
crushing it.

(b)   THE INTEGRATION OF OPPOSING FORCES: At
this level Nkrumah seemed to be operating as if he
was essentially Ghana. He misinterpreted or was
simply unaware of a vast amount cf information
about the contradictions of his own political
ideas and his acticns.   Had he succeeded in
perceiving these contradictions in thought and
action and had proceeded to explain them, he would
have had no difficulty; that is, Ghanaians would
likely have adapted to his political ideas, or
would have been perceived as adapting.

However, Nkrumah had a great deal of trouble
grappling with reality.   He was extremely
dependent upon the people but had little
understanding of their needs. Thusm he was at a
great disadvantage in grappling with basic
problems.   He was overwhelmed by his own
ideclogical predisposition and assumed the
character of a platonic "philoscpher king".   He
made no real attempts to sclve the basic problems,
but rather he minimized their effects.   Being
unclear about himself and his relationships with
the people and his cabinet, Nkrumah, at Stage I,
was unable to fix blame for the difficulties he
faced and felt caught and buffeted about without
knowing why.

He also had difficulty in making fine distinctions between reality and fantasy. He struggled to maintain the feelings cf political cmnipotence he had acquired since 1948 when he captured the imagination of every Ghanaian. At the extreme, Nkrumah, at this stage, approached something nearer to the Messianic ccmplex.23

Inappropriate as these adjustments were, Nkrumah did not submit to any type cf control, postponement of any program, cr recognize dependence on the people. He made no efforts to understand a different point of view, for he did not recognize any other pcint of view.

STAGE 2 - 1961-62: At Stage 2 is found the differentiaticn between the C.P.P. and the oppositicn into allegiants and non-allegiants with some approximation of the characteristics of each.

(a) COGNITION: Having beccme aware of allegiant and ncn-allegiant groups, Nkrumah became ccncerned with the problem of how to ccntrol non-allegiant grcups. This prcblem was focused upon with the gradual awareness of the ccmposition of the ncn-allegiant group. But he refused to admit that the ideological issues in Ghana alsc served as barriers to any form of political reconciliation with the oppositicn. While he continued to deal with the allegiant group as if it were a coherent group, he found that interactions with the tcp hierarchy of the civil service, the police, and army officers, were relatively more reliable and predictable from experience to experience, while interactions with the allegiant group were more variable and, therefore, less predictable.24

He was not yet aware of the feelings of the people, kncwing only that the pecple were somewhat different from party activists in their interaction with him. At this stage, the people were seen as kinds of "means-cbjects" to "end-objects" and, as such, only gradually acquired a new character and importance. Therefore, dependence on the people had· been denied, and theoretical speculaticns had dcminated his relaticnship with the political and social envircnments. But because of new experience, he was faced with the fact that the political system was not meeting the demands cf the people; and because of this new cognition, and consequent lack of infcrmaticn about the system's demands, he felt uncertain about his own ability tc predict the reactions of the people to the political system. It was at this time that he said to the Ministers and Party functionaries in his address at the Ideological Institute on February 3, 1962, that "they should keep contact with their staff by visiting their offices as often as possible, having homely chats with them and making them appreciate the fact that, no matter the difference in official status, a Minister and a messenger are both Ghanaians and both human beings. I am not advocating negative familiarity: that only spells ruin. What I am advocating is the cultivation of a sincere interest in one another as fellow beings, and arising from that, a mutual interest in the welfare of the State." And then he added, "Go to the people, live among them, learn from them, love them, serve them..." However, through a procedure of trial and error, he sought answers to this or that problem, attempting to find particular people, even from the non-allegiant group, who could play certain roles, for example, economists, bankers, statisticians, to make the system a viable one.

Although he had moved beyond his earlier feelings of political omnipotence, he was engaged in a process of self-examination and operated with an essentially charismatic approach to politics. But, and this was the paradox, he saw the people only in terms of his and the system's needs and felt that something was wrong with some of these means-objects, i.e., the people, who did not give the system the support it required and, therefore, he blamed the non-allegiant group and some individuals within the allegiant group for the difficulties and deprivations which arose in the system.

An indication that Nkrumah was seriously concerned about this was given on February 3, 1962, in his address at the Ideological Institute when he said, "Nothing can be more disastrous, both to the individual and to the State, than a man who becomes so discouraged in his work and so negative in his attitude to life that he carries out his duties like an automaton-disinterested. He acts like an automaton because he is treated like one. So little interest is taken in the work he turns out that he shrugs his shoulders and says, 'Why should I bother? I get paid for it'. After all, he is human."

(b) THE INTEGRATION OF OPPOSING FORCES: At this level, Nkrumah operated within a frame of reference which tended to perceive the non-allegiant group as only slightly different from the allegiant group. In his organization of the political system, these groups acted only as aids or obstacles to the realization of his programs. Those who were integrated into the system at this level faced life with Nkrumah's full support, that of the party and that of the Government, and they in turn, expected everyone to support the system so long as Nkrumah's overwhelming support was forthcoming. But Nkrumah felt that he must communicate his ideas to the non-integrated as well as the integrated, but became baffled when his ideas were not immediately accepted. When he felt deprived of the acceptance of his ideas by the non-integrated, i.e., the bulk of the educated class, his ruthlessness became even more severe because he felt the political system was threatened.

In his need to master the political situation, the allegiant and non-allegiant groups, and the people in general, he frequently fell into a pattern of crude manipulation tending to use the people as tools without regard for consequences to them, to himself, or to the system.

STAGE 3 - 1963-1964: At Stage 3 there were rules or formulae governing the relationships between the associational, non-associational, and anomic groups, with a beginning awareness of the potential for complex political manipulation.25

(a) COGNITION: Shortly after Nkrumah made the differentiation between the allegiant and non-allegiant groups, he became aware of the relationships between the associational, non-associational, and anomic groups within the political system. These groups were simply categorized by Nkrumah in terms of the role they fulfilled, i.e. keeping the workers in line with party programs and keeping the farmers informed of the Government's policies. At this level these groups were eventually emasculated and were replaced with the substitute and symbolic activities of a chosen few who operated within the framework of the C.P.P. party machinery. These few leaders were brought closer to the systemic demands and to what was described to them as being reasonable, realistic, acceptable and ideologically sound.26

They were taught, both explicitly and implicitly, that definite rules govern the relationship between the Party and the groups they have been chosen to represent, and that these rules emanated from the people. With this device he transferred the magic of the people to the magic of rules. Rules were now seen as being the magical talismans of political control and manipulation.

At this level Nkrumah operated on the assumption that associational and non-associational, and anomic groups, if not auxiliary branches of the party, were not in the interest of the political system.

(b) INTEGRATION OF THE GROUPS INTO THE C.P.P.: As of 1960, the C.P.P. was built upon the premise that the nation-building process was a process of rigidly organized, rule-bound relationships, and the leader of the party must be intensely concerned with what he must do so that he could make people respond positively to him and to the Party's program.

Nkrumah understood the behavior of the people purely as a reflection of his own manipulations and sought for final and absolute social rules which would define exactly what was expected of these groups by the political system and what they must avoid in order not to offset the balance of the system. Thus, as always, Nkrumah controlled and manipulated others without being controlled or manipulated by anyone else.

STAGE 4 - 1965: At Stage 4, Nkrumah perceived the influence of others within the system.

(a) COGNITION: Nkrumah was now prepared to see himself in new and more objective terms. His political ideas were primarily influenced by the needs of the system, but he was also aware of the influence of others and of their expectations of him. At this point, political anxiety began to emerge as a motivating force. He had accepted the impossibility of completely controlling or manipulating every segment of Ghanaian society.27 Now he was faced with the problem of being, after all, only one powerful political figure in a system filled with lesser political figures. Wanting the approval and support of these lesser figures, he submitted his actions to the criteria

of their response to him. He tried to see himself
as others saw him, attempting to predict their
reactions toward him.

Having thus accepted what others felt was
right and wrong, Nkrumah was caught in the
conflict of wanting to be like significant others
and at the same time wanting to give expression to
his own political ideas. Further, in trying to
play the role of the hero, he added to his
difficulties, essentially because he did not see
the role behavior he was playing as part of a
total organization having unique personal
consistency. In addition, because of his own
conscious manipulation of his role behavior, some
internalization took place and when he failed to
live up to the image of the 1950's, he again felt
threatened by the oppositionists.

(b) INTEGRATION OF RELATIVITY, MOVEMENT AND
     CHANGE:
At this last stage, when he perceived the
influence of others within the political system,
Nkrumah did not only become aware of this
phenomenon, but also began to comprehend more
fully the problem of order and stability and of
the integrating processes in a transitional
society. At previous stages, he had developed a
careful mastery for shifting roles and maintaining
a precarious political balance. Now, along with
increased awareness of the problems of social
change and political development and of the
processes of national integration, he began to
gain some perspective on how to deal with these
problems.28 Even with this new frame of
reference, Nkrumah still continued to seek
absolute solutions and failed to see a variety of
ways of finding a solution to the problems of
social change, stability and national integration.
This development at Stage 4 greatly diminished his
capacity for understanding and dealing with the
non-allegiant group and other groups within the
political system who were functioning at levels of
national integration and finding solutions to the
problem of social change and political development
other than his own solution.

This effort to understand the interpersonal
stages of maximizing political power in Ghana
between 1960 and 1965, is not presented as a
complete explanation of the method Nkrumah
followed; rather it is offered as a first step.
It may, indeed, appear premature, if not
oversimplified, to say that this analysis is

conclusive.29 We have only attempted to suggest a
number of generalizations which appear to us to
have a bearing on the political leadership of
Nkrumah. These generalizations do not suggest a
theory or model of power maximization in
transitional societies. If in this analysis we
have suggested preliminary approaches to analyzing
the political behavior of transitional leaders,
the seemingly psychological character of this
analysis should not be mistaken as an attempt to
postulate a methodology of power maximization in
transitional societies.

In any event, whether this analysis provides
a satisfactory interpretation of the techniques of
power maximization in Ghana between 1960 and 1965,
the conclusions arrived at, though tentative and
subject to further empirical verification, provide
us with a set of specific and concrete problems
faced by Nkrumah, i.e., the problems of societal
stability, social change and political
development.

What we have attempted to do in this chapter
was to construct from the assemblage of events and
processes a coherent picture of Nkrumah's method
of attempting to maximize his political power. In
doing so, we have based our analysis and
interpretation on observations of the moves of
Nkrumah, and on the subsequent changes that
followed the moves.

Some of the observations presented in this
chapter are doubtless common knowledge--although
they are by no means commonly acknowledged. At
times even the most simple and familiar phenomena
take on a new aspect when seen, not in isolation,
but in the context of a broader stream of events.
Our main emphasis has been on the correlations
between events and processes which, at first
glance, may seem far apart and unrelated. These
events and processes have, as far as I know,
scarcely been studied methodically. Yet they are,
so it seems to us, the basic and the most
difficult problems Nkrumah had to deal with.

REFERENCES

1.   Karl Loewenstein, MAX WEBER'S POLITICAL
      IDEAS IN THE PERSPECTIVE OF OUR TIME
      (Amherst, 1966), pp. 79-90.

2.   Max Weber, THEORY OF SOCIAL AND ECONOMIC
      ORGANIZATION (New York, 1947), p. 359.

3.   Max Weber: ESSAYS IN SOCIOLOGY, trans.
      H.H. Gerth and C.W. Mills (New York,
      1946), p. 359.

4.   Karl Loewenstein, MAX WEBER'S POLITICAL
      IDEAS, p. 74.

5.   See Benjamin. Rivlin, "The Concept of
      Political System in the Study of
      Developing States", ORBIS, X, 2 (Summer,
      1966), pp. 548-563.

6.   Monroe Berger et al., eds. "The Problem
      of Authority", FREEDOM AND CONTROL IN
      MODERN SOCIETY (1954), pp. 71-72.

7.   Gabriel A. Almond, "A Developmental
      Approach to Political Systems", WORLD
      POLITICS (January, 1965), p. 185.

8.   Apter, GHANA IN TRANSITION, p. 305.

9.   Martin Kilson, "African Autocracy",
      AFRICA TODAY (April, 1966) p. 4.

10.   W. Howard Wriggins, "Aggregation of
      Power-An Approach to Politics in
      Emerging Countries". INTERNATIONAL
      STUDIES ASSOCIATION PROCEEDINGS (April,
      1965), p. 18.

11.   Ibid., p. 119.

12.   Ibid., p. 19.

13.   Nkrumah, NEO-COLONIALISM.

14.   Ibid., p. 20.

15.   Ibid.

16.   "Social Structure and Ruling Class",
      BRITISH JOURNAL OF SOCIOLOGY (1950), p.
      10. See also Lester G. Seligman,
      LEADERSHIP IN A NEW NATION: POLITICAL
      DEVELOPMENT IN ISRAEL (New York, 1964);
      "Political Recruitment and Party
      Structure", and "The Study of Political
      Leadership", THE AMERICAN POLITICAL
      SCIENCE REVIEW, LV, I (1961), p. 77;
      "The Study of Political Leadership", THE

AMERICAN POLITICAL SCIENCE REVIEW, (XLIV (1950), pp. 904-15.

17. Hobbes, LEVIATHAN, Chap. VIII.

18. W. Albig, PUBLIC OPINION (1939), pp. 108-118.

20. See Herbert H. Hyman, POLITICAL SOCIALIZATIONS: A Study in the Psychology of Political Behavior (1959), pp. 25-91, for a number of studies done in this field.

21. C.W. Mills, SOCIOLOGICAL IMAGINATION (New York, 1959), p. 161.

22. This distinction became important in the summer of 1960, after the attempted general strike of the Trades Union Congress.

23. At this point the party press began referring to him as a messiah, redeemer, and subsequently the official designation of the Osagyefo (meaning "hero") was conferred upon him in 1960.

24. For instance, Nkrumah relied very heavily on the following: Alex Quaison-Sackey, John K. Tettehgah, Tamiah Adamafio, all of whom occupied key positions in the government.

25. The character of these groups as Nkrumah perceived them, "is the guiding force of our Ghanaian life and existence and constitutes the bulwark against national treachery, intrigue, subversion and other un-Ghanaian activities." Nkrumah, address at the Ideological Institute; Accra, Ghana (undated).

26. As Nkrumah has stated, all of these groups, The Trades Union Congress, The United Ghana Farmers Council, The National Council of Ghana Women, The Ghana Young Pioneers, and The Co-operative Movement "have their various functions in the particular aspect of our national life in which they operate, but there is one strain running through all of them which is basic and

fundamental, namely the membership of the Convention People's Party. Whatever they do, the character of the Convention People's Party must be clearly manifested for all to see. They all have a single guiding light, the guiding light of our Party ideology. This light must constantly be kept bright and full of lustre and must on no account be allowed to dim, for, as soon as this happens, we are bound to find ourselves in difficulties." Ibid. That all these groups were not able to exercise a moderating influence on the polity at a time when Ghana was not yet a monolithic elitist society and allowed Nkrumah and the C.P.P. to completely dominate the political process and to exercise an unlimited power is the key to understanding the nature of Ghanaian society. The blame must be placed squarely on the passivity of the disengaged intellectuals and an ugly sea of moral laxity. For a different point of view, see Joan Bellamy, "African Elites--A Study of Ghana", Marxism (February, 1967), pp. 37-43.

27. As if he were extending a welcoming hand to the Right Opposition and the traditional elites, he stated in a speech at a rally held in the National Assembly in Accra on June 12, 1965, to mark the 16th Anniversary of the Convention People's Party: "Comrades, in order to attain our noble and desirable ideals for Ghana and Africa, we must face up to those defects and deficiencies that militate against their realization. Here in Ghana at the present time, there seems to be a lowering in our appreciation of moral standards and spiritual values, neglect of our traditional values of chastity, purity, respect for womanhood and respect for our elders. We are doing everything to revive our culture. But if this revival is to endure, it must be solidly based on strong moral and spiritual foundations. Our moral and spiritual qualities should not lag behind the progress we are making in the economic field..."

28. In his speech, supra, p. 104, he made
this strong statement: "I must here
make special reference to the men and
women who hold key positions in the
Civil Service, corporations, and other
public services and State institutions.
SERVANTS OF THE STATE MUST BE PIONEERS.
They must show initiative and
constructive leadership in their work.
Bureaucracy, red-tapism, and the slow
moving methods of work should be
eradicted from their system once and for
all. The nation in its revolutionary
march will no longer tolerate public
officers and officials who by their
inefficiency, sluggishness, laziness and
indiferrence become a drag on us in our
march to progress." And in what was to
be the last anniversary of the C.P.P.,
he concluded, "Countrymen, the task
ahead is great indeed, and heavy is the
responsibility. And yet, it is a noble
and glorious challenge--a challenge
which calls for the courage to dream,
the courage to believe, the courage to
dare, the courage to do, the courage to
envision, the courage to fight, the
courage to work, the courage to
achieve--to achieve the highest
excellencies and the fullest greatness
of man. Dare we ask for more in life?"

29. For another historical analysis and
interpretation of Nkrumah's techniques
of maximizing political power, see David
E. Apter, "Nkrumah's Charisma, and the
Coup", DAEDALUS (Summer 1968), pp. 757-
792.

THE ROLE OF THE PARTY AS AN AGENT OF
SOCIAL CHANGE

The significance of Nkrumah's proposals for social and political transformation of Ghana lies not in their glowing promise of things to come, but rather in the use of the Convention People's Party and education as vehicles of change. This chapter examines the role of the party, as seen by Nkrumah, in the processes of social transformation of Ghana.

In his speech at the Accra Arena to celebrate the tenth anniversary of the founding of the Convention People's Party on June 12, 1959, Nkrumah defined the aim of the C.P.P. in the context of the overall transformation of Ghanaian society:

> The aim of our party is to develop our economy, modernize our agriculture and industrialize Ghana from a system of colonial economy and create a system of independent economy. Our ultimate objective is the creation of a socialist society, for we believe that only in such a society will our people have the opportunity of making the maximum contribution to the wealth, happiness and prosperity of our society as a whole.1

In the process of social transformation and political development in Ghana, Nkrumah envisioned the C.P.P. as the vanguard of the people and categorically stated that "The Convention People's Party is Ghana. Our Party not only provides the Government but is also the custodian which stands guard over the welfare of the people."2 In essence, Nkrumah seems to be suggesting that the C.P.P. is the concrete expression of the broad masses of the people. What is being denied here is the existence of an opposition party as well as the self-restraint of political parties--the very essence of democracy in the Anglo-Saxon world.

It was not hard for Nkrumah to envisage a democracy without political differences. He felt that these differences can be accommodated within a one-party system and that deviations to the "right" or to the "left" will be tolerated. This, he vehemently argued, wa s the real essence of democracy.

> The Convention People's Party is in structure democratic and socialistic in philosophy....The Party gains strength with the masses if it practices inner Party democracy and self-criticism. All members of our Party should be encouraged in every possible way to take an active part in discussing all major questions of Party life. If this is done, it will follow conclusively that all decisions of the Party are decisions of the entire membership who will correctly understand and appreciate them. Democracy will then be at its plenitude....3

An indication that Nkrumah envisioned social transformation and political development in Ghana as being possible only through the mechanisms of a one-party system and the Convention People's Party as an agent of change, was given in 1958, when he said:

> We in Africa will evolve forms of government rather different from the traditional Western pattern but no less democratic in their protection of the individual and his inalienable rights.4

This statement was eventually given a so-called "philosophical" concreteness in CONSCIENCISM in 1964, when Nkrumah wrote:

> A people's parliamentary democracy with a one-party system is better able to express and satisfy the common aspirations of a nation as a whole, than a multiple-party parliamentary system, which is in fact only a ruse for perpetuating, and covers up, the inherent struggle between the "haves" and the "have-nots".5

Nkrumah sees the emergence of the one-party system as quite natural under certain conditions. The first condition is that independence from colonial dependency should bring into power the "extremists" of the independence movement who demanded political freedom as the key to social change and political development; the second condition is that since the "extremists" and not the "moderates" of the professional class and the traditional elites won independence, the party of the "extremists" must become the protector of the people as well as the instrument for social change. Given these two sets of conditions, the opposition party would dwindle and would soon cease to be a political force of any consequence.

We must hasten to point out that if these sets of conditions as given by Nkrumah are present in any modernizing society, there can be no reason for a two-party system; for the opposition party must demand a return to colonial subjugation which the people have already rejected. In the alternative, the opposition party will confine its claims to remaining a political party by its ability to perform more efficiently tasks being carried out by the "extremists" party. But this chance is remote as Nkrumah has argued that this is a function which could quite easily be performed within the "extremists" party, i.e., the party for national liberation. Nkrumah has made this point quite clear:

If the will of the people is democratically expressed in an overwhelming majority for the governing party, and thereby creates a weakening of the accepted two-party pattern...the government is obliged to respect the will of the people so expressed. We have no right to divide our mandate in defiance of the popular will.6

If, therefore, the party is the vanguard of the people and the historic agent of social change and political development in Ghana, what are the basic principles underlying Nkrumah's concept of the Party in the process of social change? Our analysis of his writings with particular reference to the C.P.P. reveals these five basic principles.

First, the party membership must be broadened to embrace all the people; the people's welfare must be the overriding priority of the party. In the process of social change and political development in Ghana, Nkrumah argued that there is a need for a new political party: "A new Party, militant, dynamic and revolutionary had to be formed to mobilize the chiefs and people into a force capable of turning the scales in our favor."7

Secondly, the party in leading the struggle for national social transformation and political development must have a consistent program and an ideology; "an ideology whose aim shall be to contain the African experience of Islamic and Euro-Christian experience as well as the experience of the traditional African society, and, by gestation, employ them for the harmonious growth and development of that society."8 This ideology must not be merely a "conceptual refutation of a dying social order, but a positive creative theory, the guiding light of the emerging social order."9 And a link is established between a program and an ideology--the ideology postulates the general theoretical framework to be followed by the party while the program outlines the targets and tasks of the party at any given moment of the struggle for social transformation. The editors of THE SPARK have argued that

It would be wrong to have a program without an ideology. For as conditions change, it becomes necessary to change the program. And an attempt to draw up a program, if there is no ideology to guide the action, may lead to a break-up of the party. This danger is ever present in a party whose membership is open to all, irrespective of social and economic status.10

Thirdly, if the party must continue to be the vanguard of the people and the agent of social change and political development, education of party members must be given top priority. Since the party is presumed to be a mass party, in order to effectively put the programs of the party into operation, "great reliance must be placed on party education as the instrument for welding this amorphous collection of people into an organic and dedicated body of men and women sharing an identical view of human society."11 To attain this important objective, "every avenue of education and information must be used to stir and nourish the political consciousness of the people."12 This third principle led to the establishment of an ideological institute at Winneba, where party functionaries received a crash course in "general political education". The educational work of the institute was supplemented with party activists in factories and farms. As Nkrumah put it, "Party study groups exist all over the country, in factories, workshops, government departments, and offices, in fact, in every nook and cranny of Ghana, for the study of African life and culture, party ideology,

decisions and programs, and for explaining
government policies and actions."13

where party functionaries received a crash course
in "general political education". policies and
actions."13

Fourthly, the party must be a disciplinary
party with a strong sense of dedication and
leadership. The organizational principle of the
party must be "democratic centralism". In the
party all must be equal regardless of race or
tribe and must be free to express their views.
"But once a majority decision is taken, we expect
such a decision to be loyally executed, even by
those who must have opposed that decision. This
we consider and proclaim to be the truest form of
Democratic Centralism-decisions freely arrived at
and loyally executed."14

Fifthly, the supremacy of the party over
other functional institutions in Ghana must be
upheld by all party members regardless of their
position. In all things political, the party must
be given priority because it is the revolutionary
vanguard of the people and the only effective
agent of social transformation and political
development. In the process of social
transformation the government is but a handmaiden
of the party. Nkrumah made this point
categorically clear when he stated:

I want it to be firmly understood that
it is the Convention People's Party which
makes the Government and not the Government
which makes the Convention People's Party,
and we intend to give public acknowledgement
to this fact by raising the prestige of our
Party to its proper status in our national
structure.15

One of the characteristics of social
engineering in a modernizing society is for the
political leadership, or the "masters of social
engineering" to refrain from seeking an emotional
mass following, because the natural modus operandi
of the masses is "direct action", which is not
necessarily positive and constructive. Our
analysis indicates that Nkrumah was much more
interested in revolutionary rhetoric than
programmatic action. In fact, the whole approach
of the party was based on these five notions:

1.   Belief in the revolutionary ability of the masses;

2.   Organization of the masses around their needs and aspirations;

3.   Learning about the masses by living with them;

4.   Leading the masses into action to fight for their own demands;

5.   Indissoluble ties with all the organizations of the masses.16

although by 1960 the C.P.P. had ceased to be a mass-based party. By this time party membership was restricted. Individuals seeking to become party members had to pass through a series of tests before being accepted into the ranks of the party. The local party branches became party educational centers; and an applicant for party membership had to attend lectures on party ideology and demonstrate his understanding of Nkrumaism before being considered for membership. The party was no longer the party with which the masses identified themselves. But Nkrumah still continued to use the same political rhetoric he used in 1949--"The strength of the organized masses is invincible....We must organize as never before, for organization decides everything."17 By 1963 it seemed to have dawned on him that the C.P.P. was no longer a mass-based political party. It was in recognition of this fact that a renewed effort was launched to widen the membership of the party. Speaking before the party members at the 14th anniversary of the C.P.P. on June 12, 1963, he stated:

> Our Party must ever be concerned with multiplying and strengthening its contacts with the masses of the people and winning their confidence as their defenders against the evils of poverty, disease, hunger, ignorance and squalor to whose elimination we are dedicated.18

But the damage had already been done. The C.P.P. had ceased to be a mass-based party. It was left for Nkrumah to devise a new strategy since it had become clear that the party was no longer capable of acting as the historic agent of change in society. It was in this vein that

Nkrumah created the people's militia in 1964. At
this point Nkrumah shifted his strategy from using
the party to transform Ghanaian society to a
strategy which subsumed that the revolutionary
struggle for social change and political
development can only be activated by a fusion of
political-military organizations. "Revolutionary
politics, if they are not to be blocked, must be
diverted from politics as such. Political
resources must be thrown into an organization
which is simultaneously political and military,
transcending all existing polemics."19   Thus,
Nkrumah has argued, that "If armed militia are not
organized, the masses cannot manifest their power
in the struggle against the enemy", and that "As
the people's revolutionary struggle advances,
professional armies as such will gradually
disappear..."20

     The C.P.P., Nkrumah claimed, was "imbued with
Marxist Socialist philosophy."21   But in the
process of trying to actualize its socialist
objectives, it failed to live up to its stated
goals and historic mission. The party thrived on
bribery., corruption and nepotism.22   But,
nevertheless, Nkrumah was determined to maintain
the outward appearance of the C.P.P. which for all
practical purposes was dead as a political party.
Though he regards himself as a Marxist-Leninist,
he did not heed their revolutionary injunction, as
stated by Regis Debray:

          Marxist-Leninist parties which do not
     fulfill their revolutionary obligations   must
     be prevented from setting themselves up as
     associations for the protection of threatened
     interests, thereby impeding the inevitable
     rise of new forms of organization and
     revolutionary action. By the name they bear
     and the ideology they proclaim, they occupy
     de jure the place of the popular vanguard; if
     they do not occupy it de facto, they must not
     be permitted to keep the post vacant. There
     is no exclusive ownership of the
     revolution.23

     By the end of Nkrumah's regime, both de facto
and de jure, the C.P.P. had ceased to occupy the
place of the popular vanguard of the people. It
became dictatorial and more bourgeois than the
Right Opposition.

Thus far we have noted the eclecticism of Nkrumah's theories concerning the role of the single party as the vanguard of the people and as the historic agent of social transformation. We have also noted the tactical failures of Nkrumah in using the C.P.P. to lead the struggle for social transformation. But Nkrumah's failure and his subsequent overthrow must not be mistaken as an indication of the impracticability of the one-party system. The Anglo-Saxon notion that democracy requires the existence of an organized opposition to the Government does not only seem irrelevant but also empirically false. How can leaders in modernizing societies transfer mechanically institutions developed in differentiated Western industrial societies to societies whose conditions are structurally different? How can an organized opposition to the Government continue to exist when there is only one party that embodies the common aspirations of the masses, and which the overwhelming majority of the masses continually votes for? The C.P.P. did not become dominant solely because of the popularity of Nkrumah. It represented the popular choice.

A legitimate criticism may be directed against Nkrumah for confusing the positive principles of Anglo-Saxon liberal democracy with the unworkable and cumbersome parliamentary institutions and procedures that traditionally embody these principles. However, the basic sociological facts that contributed to monocentricism and authoritarianism in Ghana are backwardness, ethnicity and the legacy of colonialism which engendered opposition to tribalism and a movement devoted to national consolidation. Sociologically, social backwardness inevitably means a low level of political sophistication--and in a society with a very simple social structure, the dominant political force is more likely to assume total power. But in such a society with a monocentric government, there are, indeed, dangers inherent in the very nature of the one-party system. Julius Nyerere, President of Tanzania, has, indeed pointed out the negative aspects of the one-party system in less differentiated societies:

Of course, such overwhelming social unity has its dangers. But the danger lies not in the absence of an artificially created opposition organization, but in the possible

exclusion of the eccentric, the one who does
not conform to the social mores. It is by
the existence of a place for the "odd man
out" that a newly independent country can be
judged to be fully democratic....He must not
only be allowed to live without any
restriction on his personal freedom; he must
be able to contribute to his society through
his work and ideas. The all-pervading,
nation-building nationalist organization must
be able to incorporate and use the man who
deliberately stands apart from its
institutions.24

However tractable the one-party system may
seem to leaders of transitional societies, very
often internal restraints on single-party
authoritarianism are virtually absent. In Ghana,
it was world opinion that exercised the most
important influence over Nkrumah's actions. But
it must also be pointed out that in traditional
Ghanaian society, social institutions viewed by
Marxists as the outcome of conflict between
particular interest groups within society, were
eschewed. Instead, traditional elders preached
complementarity and the harmonization of sectional
interests in order to attain the higher interests
of society as a whole. Consequently, the people
are regarded as the fount of instinctive natural
reason--thus the traditional elders never alienate
themselves from the people. They immerse
themselves in, and become co-extensive with the
people. It was also because of this sociological
fact of traditional democratization in Ghana
acting as an important countervailing check on the
unrestrained activities of the C.P.P. and Nkrumah,
that led to the failure of Nkrumah in using the
C.P.P. as an agent of social transformation in
Ghana. In trying to use the C.P.P. as an agent of
social transformation, Nkrumah emasculated some of
the traditional authorities and replaced them with
party activists. But in the process of winning
the allegiance of the people these party activists
had to identify themselves with the traditional
values of the people. In so doing they became
more traditional than the traditional authorities.
Thus they were unable to perform the tasks for
which they were recruited.

The failure of Nkrumah to use the C.P.P. as
the vehicle of social transformation does not
minimize the contributions of the C.P.P. toward
the eventual detribalization of Ghana at least

during Nkrumah's rule. Contrary to the popularly
held view of Nkrumah as a dictator, it is our
contention that his view of the party as the
vanguard of the people and as the only instrument
of meaningful transformation in Ghana is the
proper view. A one-party system in transitional
societies brings about the genuine unity of a
country, otherwise diversified. A one-party
system is a response to decolonization and social
transformation. Within it are democratic aims and
a praxis of democracy in a non-Anglo-Saxon
context. Julius Nyerere has indeed drawn a fine
distinction between democracy African style and
democracy Anglo-Saxon style:

> This idea of "for" and "against", this
> obsession with "Government" balanced by
> "Official Opposition"...though it may exist
> in a democracy, is not essential to it,
> although it happens to have become so
> familiar to the Western World that its
> absence immediately raises the cry
> "Dictatorship".

> I consider to be essential to
> democractic government: discussion,
> equality, and freedom....Those who doubt the
> African's ability to establish a democratic
> society cannot seriously be doubting the
> African's ability to "discuss". That is the
> one thing that is as African as the tropical
> sun. Neither can they be doubting the
> African's sense of equality....Traditionally,
> the African knows no class....

> If democracy, then, is a form of
> government freely established by the people
> themselves, and if its essentials are free
> discussion and equality, there is nothing in
> traditional African society which unfits the
> African for it. On the contrary, there is
> everything in his tradition which fits the
> African to be just what he claims he is, a
> natural democrat....

> To the Anglo-Saxon tradition, the two-
> party system has become the very essence of
> democracy. It is no use telling an Anglo-
> Saxon that when a village of a hundred people
> have sat and talked together until they
> agreed where a well should be dug, they have
> practiced democracy. The Anglo-Saxon will
> want to know whether the talking was properly

organized. He will want to know whether
there was an organized group "for" the
motion, and an equally well organized group
"against" the motion....25

Though the tradition of free discussion is a
force restraining monocentrism, there are those
who would argue that since African society is
socially and politically backward and less
sophisticated in socio-economic and political
matters, free discussion would necessarily be on a
low level, thus, it would not have any restraining
influence on monocentricism. Usually, Soviet
experience of "democratic centralism" is cited as
an example. But empirical evidence seems to
indicate that free expression and discussion of
issues exercise a liberalizing influence on
authoritarian regimes.

Democracy, however important to the Anglo-
Saxon West, is not the consideration which
determines whether a society should become
liberalized or not. What determines the course of
a nation is the courage of the leadership of the
nation and the answers as well as the
interpretations they provide for given problems
and how these are transmitted with compelling
force to the people.

REFERENCES

1. AXIOMS OF KWAME NKRUMAH (London, 1967),
   pp. 42-43.
2. Ibid., p. 42.

3. Ibid., pp. 45-46.

4. Nkrumah, Speech to the Indian Council on
   World Affairs, December 26, 1958.

5. CONSCIENCISM, (London, 1964), p. 101.

6. NKRUMAH, AFRICA MUST UNITE, p. 71.

7. Nkrumah, Address to the National
   Assembly, June 12, 1965.

8. Nkrumah, CONSCIENCISM, p. 70.

9. Ibid., p. 34.

10. SOME ESSENTIAL FEATURES OF NKRUMAISM, pp. 92-93.

11. Ibid., p. 93.

12. Nkrumah, AFRICA MUST UNITE, p. 130.

13. Ibid., p. 131.

14. Nkrumah, Speech at the Accra Arena to celebrate the tenth anniversary of the founding of the C.P.P., June 12, 1959.

15. Speech made in Accra, June 12, 1960, cited in AXIOMS OF KWAME NKRUMAH, p. 43.

16. SOME ESSENTIAL FEATURES OF NKRUMAISM, pp. 98-99.

17. Accra EVENING NEWS (January 14, 1949), cited in SOME ESSENTIAL FEATURES OF NKRUMAISM, p. 99.

18. Cited in AXIOMS, p. 46.

19. Regis Debray, REVOLUTION IN THE REVOLUTION (New York, 1967), p. 124.

20. Nkrumah, AXIOMS, p. 109.

21. Nkrumah, AFRICA MUST UNITE, p. 129.

22. See Nkrumah, "Dawn Broadcast", (April 8, 1961), in which he chastised party functionaries for not setting good examples to be emulated by the people.

23. Regis Debray, op. cit., p. 125.

24. Julius Nyerere, "The Future of African Nationalism", TRIBUNE (London, May 27, 1960).

25. Quoted by Professor Peter Worsley, THE THIRD WORLD, pp. 207-208.

THE ROLE OF EDUCATION IN SOCIAL CHANGE

Our purpose here is to examine the changes
that were introduced by Nkrumah in the Ghanaian
educational system. It is beyond the ambit of
this book to spin a web between the attitudes of
mind in the European tradition of education and
the European tradition of education as exported to
the colonies. Nor are we interested in the
historical perspective in political, economic, and
social background of educational development in
the colonies. Other studies have dealt
extensively with these problems.1

In the pre-independence colonial period "The
wholesale transfer of the educational conventions
of Europe and America to the peoples of Africa has
certainly not been an act of wisdom, however
justly it may be defended as a proof of genuine
interest in the native people."2 Elementary
education was narrowly literary; and secondary
education was predominantly classical and was
exclusively geared to the conventional
requirements of university admission and the
Colonial Civil Service.

But with the emergence of nationalism in the
post-World War II era, education became a major
concern of the nationalist leaders. It became
critically clear to them that in the modernization
process, i.e. the technological and economic
transformation of society, with growing social
mobility, meaningful education must be given
priority. Since education is the motive force of
social improvement and modernization, it became
politicized and the political party in control of
the government turned to the educational system
for political indoctrination, as well as a means
of narrowing the economic gaps. But in order to
narrow these horizons, a change in consciousness
must occur; this change, if it is to occur, must
occur as a result of enlightened education.
Nkrumah, speaking on this subject, said:

Education consists not only in the sum
of what a man knows, or the skill with which
he can put this to his own advantage. In my

view, a man's education must also be measured
in terms of the soundness of his judgment of
people and things, and in his power to
understand and appreciate the needs of his
fellowmen, and to be of service to them. The
educated man should be (so) sensitive to the
conditions around him that he makes it his
chief endeavor to improve those conditions
for the good of all.3

It should be pointed out that Nkrumah made a
deliberate attempt to use the educational
systemto foster modernization and social
transformation. In this sense, education was
made available to all--and the institutions
were required to set an example:

We have been doing a great deal to make
education available to all. It is equally
important that education should seek the
welfare of the people and recognize our
attempts to solve our economic, cultural,
technological and scientific problems....We
look to the Universities to set an example by
their efficiency and their senses of
responsibility in the use of public funds.
They must also set an example in loyalty to
the Government and the people, in good
citizenship, public morality and behavior.4

It is not difficult to understand the demands
placed on the universities by Nkrumah when we look
at the pattern of higher education in Ghana in the
colonial period. In organization, the
universities followed those of Britain--they were
autonomous and deliberately detached from the
government; in standards and curriculum they
stressed a thin excellence and narrow
specialization; and in social function they
regarded themselves as a privileged class. The
universities, which were all completely
residential, were to produce "men and women with
the standards of public service and capacity for
leadership which self-rule requires. In short,
they were, as in England, to nurture an elite."5
"The African wanted a replica of the British
university at its best...."6 Until 1961, when the
constitution of the University of Ghana was
changed, "The four halls of residence were made
self-governing, each with its own by-laws (no two
alike) and its officers: Master, Senior Tutor,
Chaplain, Steward to High Table. As in Cambridge,
the halls and not the university accountant
collected the students' fees. The terms (in a
country with a considerable animist and Moslem

population) were labelled Michaelmas, Lent, and Trinity. Grace at table was read in Latin. The purchasing officer was called a manciple."7

The consequence of this educational transplantation was that very often the graduates of the University of Ghana were ill-adapted to their own social environment--the curriculum to a large extent excluded the possibility of a broad liberal education and instead stressed the honors program. From 1957-60, the faculty of Arts of the University of Ghana graduated 95 students with honors degrees in single subjects and only 45 students with general degrees in Arts.8 However, since 1960 a reasonable balance has been restored between the number of students in the general and honors degree programs. The underlying assumption of the honors degree program was the "belief that the social function of a university in Africa was to create and sustain an intellectual elite."9 Thus, those who came out of the university rarely addressed themselves to the socio-economic and political problems of the country. There was a wedge between them and the people. Eric Ashby has, indeed, pointed out that

> For an African, the impact of a University education is something inconceivable to a European. It separates him from his family and his village (though he will, with intense feeling and loyalty, return regularly to his home and accept what are often crushing family responsibilities). It obliges him to live in a Western way, whether he likes to or not. It stretches his nerve between two spiritual worlds, two systems of ethics, two horizons of thought. In his hands he holds the terrifying instrument of Western civilization: the instrument which created Jefferson's speeches, the philosophy of Marx, the mathematics and chemistry of atomic destruction. His problem is how to apply this instrument to the welfare of his own people. But he has no opportunity to reflect on this problem. For one thing, the gap between himself and his people is very great.10

The only way to bridge the gap between the educated African and his people and to change the consciousness of the elite was to change the content of the curriculum at the university level

and to create more secondary and technical schools
in which secondary and high-level applied science
and technology, i.e., agriculture, engineering,
economics, law, medicine and teacher training
would be the core of the curriculum instead of
Christian theology, Latin, Greek, geography and
ancient history. Also the content of the
curriculum must be related to the cultural ethos
of the society. And Nkrumah made it clear that
"We must in the development of our University bear
in mind that once it had been planted in African
soil it must take root amidst African traditions
and culture."11

Ironically, the opposition to changes in the
curriculum came from the African intellectuals
rather than the expatriate professors who
dominated the University Council, i.e., the
policy-making body of the university. The African
intellectuals doubted whether African studies
should have a place in a university curriculum.
Professor Ashby in his study of African
nationalism's confrontation with the African
university pointed out that:

> Some African intellectuals, especially
> those educated in Britain, resist changes in
> curriculum or in pattern of courses because
> they confuse such changes with a lowering of
> standards. They are accordingly suspicious
> of any divergence from the British pattern.
> Some of them are particularly allergic to
> proposals for incorporating African studies
> into the curriculum. Is this, they say, the
> first step toward disarming us
> intellectually; to substitute Arabic and
> African languages for the classics; to teach
> English to Africans as Chinese is taught to
> Englishmen, not as Englishmen learn English
> at Cambridge; to neglect Tudor history in
> favour of the history of Africa; to regard
> oral tradition as legitimate material for
> scholarship; to take seriously the political
> institutions of a Yoruba town; to reflect on
> the indigenous ethical system of animists and
> Moslems as well as on Christian ethics?12

In October 1961, under the direction of
Nkrumah and the government (when the state was
already playing a role in university policy), it
was announced that the Institute of African
Studies at Legon would be expanded and that all
first year undergraduate students would follow a
course in African studies "stressing the unity of
the African continent in all its aspects."13 A

two-year post-graduate course leading to a
Master's degree in African studies was established
with courses in languages; history; social,
political and economic institutions; music and
art. Nana Nketsia, head of the Institute,
commented that "For the first time since Ghana's
contact with Europe in the fifteenth century, the
two universities in Ghana are serving as places
where creative and conscious reflections on life
in Africa are being undertaken."14

Professor Conor Cruise O'Brien, then vice
chancellor of the University of Ghana, had this to
say about African studies in the University
curriculum:

> We should be very clear...that this
> tendency (to develop the Institute of African
> Studies) is not a restrictive one....Far from
> being a restriction, the development of
> interest in African studies is a liberation:
> it is a liberation from that older and
> narrower concept of a university in Africa as
> being a place whose main and virtually sole
> function was to pursue European studies and
> disseminate European knowledge in
> Africa....In transcending that narrow concept
> and in becoming more fully a part of its
> environment, an African university becomes
> not merely more fully African but also more
> fully a university.15

Before going into a statistical analysis of
the changes and improvements that occurred in the
field of education during Nkrumah's regime, let us
first examine the role of the university in Ghana
in relation to the state. In the processes of
modernization, Nkrumah did not accept the
traditional conventions of Britain which exempt
the universities from state control. The
university in the African context must provide the
desired leadership and create the attitudinal
changes needed in order to transform the society.
And, as the "Programme of the convention People's
Party for Work and Happiness" put it:

> The Party and Government are determined
> that our Universities will no longer produce
> "Ivory Tower" graduates and that Ghanaian
> boys and girls, who have had the benefit of
> the best education that the country can
> provide, will identify themselves completely
> with the cause of the people.16

Nkrumah was particularly concerned about the role of the university in a transitional society, such as Ghana, and he wanted to leave no doubt whatsoever in the minds of faculty and students alike as to what his position was. Speaking at a university dinner in 1963, he stated:

The role of a university in a country like ours is to become the academic focus of national life, reflecting the social, economic, cultural, and political aspirations of the people. It must kindle national interests in the youth and uplift our citizens and free them from ignorance, superstition, and, may I add, indolence. A university does not exist in a vacuum or in outer space. It exists in the context of a society and it is there that it has its proper place. A university is supported by society, and without the sustenance which it receives from society, it will cease to exist.17

To see why this is so--to comprehend what intellectualism and a university degree means to the Ghanaian-- we remind ourselves of what, historically, happened in Britain. The British model of a university exhibits certain components and sequences whose relevance is global. But the model evolved in Britain is not transplantable in its universal sense, and, therefore, not an historically ideal model for Ghana.

In 1960 an international commission was appointed by the government of Ghana to advise on the future development of higher education in Ghana. The commission's chairman was the Hon. Kojo Botsio, a cabinet minister in Nkrumah's government. The other members of the commission included three educators from England, two from the U.S.A., one Russian, and one African from Sierra Leone. The commission's advice on the relations between universities and the State rested on two basic principles:

a)   that Ghanaian universities "should be able to respond to the immediate and future needs of the community" and

b)   "that they should have the greatest possible autonomy in their organization, teaching, and research."18

The commission's report was accepted by the government and on July 1, 1961, a "University of

Ghana Bill" passed through Parliament.19 The Bill
set forth the criteria to be used in planning the
curriculum of the university as follows:

> In determining the subjects to be
> taught, emphasis should be placed upon those
> which are of special relevance to the needs
> and aspirations of Ghanaians, including the
> furtherance of African unity.

Then the commission's report went on to
outline the structure of the governing body of the
university:

> The principal officers of the university
> shall be the Chancellor, the Chairman of the
> University Council, and the Vice
> Chancellor...The President (of the Republic)
> shall hold the office of Chancellor and as
> such shall be the Head of the University.
> The Chairman of the University Council shall
> be appointed by the Chancellor...A person
> shall not be appointed as Vice-Chancellor
> unless his appointment has been approved by
> the Chancellor...The governing body of the
> university...shall consist of the following
> fifteen members:

> a) the principal officers of the University
> (the Chancellor, Vice-Chancellor,
> Chairman of the University Council)

> b) four persons appointed by the
> Chancellor.

> c) the secretary for the time being of the
> National Council for Higher Education
> and Research.

> d) a person elected by a body appearing to
> the Chancellor to be representative of
> heads of secondary schools.

Though the commission's report was given
qualified approval by the government, one
certainty was that Nkrumah became the head of the
University and, consequently, had ultimate control
over policy. However, the administration of the
university was left to the Academic Board.

By 1962, the Convention People's Party was
calling for re-examination of the university and a
study of the entrance requirements. In its

"Programme for Work and Happiness" it stated categorically:

> University education will be expanded to enable all who can profit from it to take advantage of the facilities for higher education provided by Government. The Party and Government propose that University Entrance Examinations shall be abolished and that the West African School Certificate shall be sufficient qualification for entry into our Universities. Accordingly, the Party proposes that the present Sixth Form courses provided in the Secondary Schools should cease and that Sixth-form work should become the first year of the four-year University course.

Nkrumah had earlier stated elsewhere that "If reforms do not come from within, we intend to impose them from outside, and no resort to the cry of academic freedom (for academic freedom does not mean irresponsibility) is going to restrain us from seeing that our University is a healthy University devoted to Ghanaian interests."[20] He went on to say that:

> It pains me to have to say that these institutions are not pulling their weight. The returns which we are getting for the money poured into these institutions is most discouraging. I have already aired my criticisms on another occasion about the Kumasi College of Technology. Let me here look at the University College. Over 90% of the student body is being maintained by Government scholarships. It costs us more to produce a graduate at Legon than in many other Universities abroad. We have provided with unparalleled lavishness all the facilities necessary. It is a common opinion that our students are "feather-bedded". And what is the result? With few exceptions University College is a breeding ground for unpatriotic and anti-Government elements. But the students are not alone to be blamed. The staff bears a heavy responsibility for the anti-Government atmosphere which prevails. We are not fools. We know all that is happening and we can pinpoint those elements, both native and foreign, around which this unhealthy state of affairs revolves.

I want my present observations to serve
as a warning. We do not intend to sit idly
by and see these institutions which are
supported by millions of pounds produced out
of the sweat and toil of the common people
continue to be the centres of anti-Government
activities.21

This concern of the head of a developing
country about the role and impact of the
university on the totality of society cannot be
vainly construed as an undue interference as is so
often heard from his critics, i.e., fastidious
academics whose only concern is with the
university. After all, the universities, like
other corporate bodies, are political microcosms
akin to the society at large.

To understand the uneasiness of the students
and the response of the government, we must take
into serious consideration the new occupational
and status aspirations of the students which were
focused on relatively restricted pre-existing
ranges of occupational and status conceptions.
The great propensity of Ghanaian graduates to
bureaucratic white-collar jobs, as against
technical, agricultural and business occupations,
and the lack of the availability of bureaucratic
white-collar jobs, these already having been
filled with C.P.P. activists, is perhaps the
clearest indication of the students' anti-
government activities.

Secondly, it seems Ghanaian graduates are
unable to adapt to the wider social setting of
their society and to engage in enterprises other
than civil service jobs. This attitude is best
exemplified by the curriculum of the university
and the type of class formation that eventuates,
i.e., the preponderance of university graduates
alienated from the society and who are in the main
absorbed into the civil service-- they are a
cohesive intelligentsia group at the very top of
society, economically and socially. Although the
university was a natural ground for anti-
Government activities and socio-political unrest,
the political activism of the students dissipated
relatively quickly once they were absorbed into
the state bureaucracies; their activism in the
main was never channeled into continuous
transformative groups in the society. Our view is
that these students were unable to continue their
political activities after leaving the university

because as students they were mainly concerned
with their careers, thus operating under false
consciousness. After graduation, they succumbed
to the pressures of the government, became
disorganized as a group, and were unable to orient
themselves to the wider spectrum of their society.

Perhaps the best starting point for judging
Nkrumah's relation with the university is an
analysis of the pattern of demands for manpower
made by the developing socio-political and
economic structure of Ghana and the attempts made
by fastidious academics to influence the process
of education, either as a selfish means of
political influence and social control of society
or as an assurance of their own socio-economic
status. They ignored the importance of education,
i.e., "identification with various cultural socio-
political symbols and values and of relatively
active commitment to various cultural, social, and
political groups and organizations."22

We must point out that the politicization of
the university governing body did not threaten or
lower the academic standards. It only made clear
that the government attached great importance to
the university as an active agent of change in the
modernization process. The criticism of Nkrumah's
interference in the affairs of the university by
the African elite is understandable because "an
education confined to providing the colonial
inhabitant with new tools could be very useful if
it left the personality as a whole untouched and
had no direct cultural import, but a culturally-
biased education can disrupt the personality far
more than one would expect."23

Now let us turn our attention to the
secondary, technical and the primary school
levels. The Party "Programme for Work and
Happiness" stated inter alia that

> Primary and Middle School
> education,...has been made compulsory and
> free. The duration of the Primary and Middle
> School courses will be reduced to eight years
> and the Secondary School courses will last
> four years. The Party proposes that
> Secondary School education will also become
> free and compulsory during the operation of
> the Seven-year Plan. Provision will
> therefore be made for the training and
> recruitment of larger numbers of teachers.

On curriculum planning, the Programme stated:

The curricula for schools will be revised so as to bring (them) more in line with our national aspirations. One of the most neglected aspects of Ghanaian education at present is, in the Party's view, Technical Education. The Party, therefore, proposes to increase the number of Institutes providing technical and vocational training; polytechnics and other institutes required for our national reconstruction. Such technical training will cover Metallurgy, Engineering, Economics, Statistics, Accountancy, and Management.

The Programme was, indeed, an ambitious one. The pattern of education envisaged was the teaching of skills needed for the economic and social reconstruction of the country. The government and party had envisaged that since the children coming out of the primary schools are only equipped with the basic skills of reading, writing and arithmetic, "facilities must be provided for them to learn the skills and attainments that will fit them for life as members of a modern labour force", thus the government "proposed to supplement the six-year course of basic primary education by a two-year course at a continuing school in which the children will be introduced to elementary skills of a more specifically economic value."24

On the secondary level of education, the students are to be given a background in technical skills and exposed to industry, agriculture, and other sectors of the economy. Students on the secondary level would receive a sound basic education so as to facilitate their work in the structure of the economy. "These people, who constitute the middle and potential high level manpower of the economy, are those of whom there is the greatest scarcity in Ghana."25 As for facilities, the government proposed that

Further training in the technical institutes and universities will be expanded to cope with an increasing volume and a rising technological level of work. At the same time, their extramural impact must be widened. Opportunities will be provided for an increasing number of working people to continue their education and training through part-time attendance, evening courses, short

intensive courses and correspondence
courses.26

Though the manpower planning proposed by the
government was sound, it did not take into account
those factors accounting for the unemployment of
primary, middle, and secondary school leavers, nor
did it suggest any action to combat it.

It is our view that in the modernization
process, and especially in manpower planning, a
modernizing society must be able to "generate
occupational structures capable of producing a
more rapid rate of economic growth than that of
the industrial countries."27

The government's seven-year plan proposed
that "Since the plan also calls for the absorption
of most of these new workers (school leavers) into
industry and modernized agriculture it is
necessary that a maximum number of them should be
fitted out by the educational system to fill jobs
that require skill and training."28 But,

> In doing so, they (the government) need
> not rely on a tried pattern of occupations,
> for the combination of tasks which make up
> each occupational category can be changed
> without necessarily changing the over-all
> description of jobs or tasks undertaken
> within the economy. To encourage people to
> relate their activities together in new
> patterns, educators, training experts, and
> those concerned primarily with the supply and
> deployment of manpower must take such changes
> into consideration in their planning.29

In working out the pattern of education
necessary for the socio-economic and political
transformation of Ghana, the government proposed
to "shorten the overall length of time required
for the completion of elementary education from
ten years as it is at present to eight years. Of
these the first six years will be devoted to the
acquisition of those basic skills of literacy that
are now taught in the six years of primary and the
first two years of middle school."30 This
proposal was purely economical. The government
had estimated that within the period of the seven-
year plan, nearly two million additional pupils
would be enrolled in the elementary schools of the
country. Unless the length of elementary
education was shortened from ten to eight years,
these pupils would not become available to the
labor force before 1970.31

The next stage is the continuing school which will accommodate the elementary school graduates who do not enter secondary schools. The continuing school is a two-year post-basic schooling in manipulative and technical skills. The Seven-Year Plan proposes that:

the continuing school curriculum will include various trades related to the industrial and construction sectors of the economy; modern agricultural techniques; typing and shorthand together with simple office routine; elementary book-keeping and accountancy... 32

The third stage is secondary and secondary technical school, which constitutes the training ground for all the high level and also much of the middle level manpower requirements of the country. 33 The introduction of free and compulsory primary education created an imbalance in the number of primary school graduates entering secondary and technical schools. To redress this imbalance, the government proposed to increase the enrollment in secondary and technical schools at the rate of 2000 pupils per year. This was expected to increase to about 80,000 by 1970. Out of this number, the yearly output of secondary and technical school graduates will rise from 3,000 to 14,000 and by 1970, 16,000 of these graduates will go on for further studies beyond the secondary and technical schools. To accomplish these objectives, the government proposed that:

the number of secondary school teachers will have to be increased from the present level of 1000 to about 4,300 by 1970. Since secondary school teachers must have a university degree or equivalent qualification and the proposed expansion in the secondary schools is itself required to take place before the Universities can begin to produce enough graduates, it is expected that in the course of the seven years there will be a large deficit of graduate teachers which will have to be made good by the recruitment of expatriate staff. After about 1965, when a higher output is expected from the universities, this deficit of graduate teachers should be gradually eliminated. Before then, however, it is estimated that about 200 additional teachers a year will

need to be recruited from outside Ghana for
about three or four years. 34

In the field of technical education, the
government proposed to train a group of "senior
technicians who stand between the engineers and
managers on the one hand and the skilled labor on
the other hand",35 men who would be responsible
for the implementation and supervision of
projects. Since the Kwame Nkrumah University of
Science and Technology has the responsibility of
training professional engineers and agronomists,
the government proposed to

> (establish) additional senior technical
> institutes to allow the enrollment of 500
> entrants per year. The training
> facilities...available in Kumasi for the
> training of technical teachers can be
> expanded to supply all the additional
> requirements for staffing these senior
> technical institutes. The institutes will be
> sited in the most suitable areas having
> regard to the developing industrial structure
> and the facilities thereby available for the
> practical training of technicians in going
> industrial and agricultural enterprises. 36

The most important aspect of the proposed
educational development is the quality of the
teaching staff of all these schools. Since the
introduction of the universal free compulsory
primary education, the quality of teaching had
dropped. By 1964, out of 32,000 primary school
teachers approximately 40% were untrained. With
the increase in primary school enrolment estimated
at about one million by 1970, only 20,000 new
teachers would have been trained by then. The
consequence would be a further lowering in the
quality of teaching. To aver t this, the
government proposed

> to increase the enrolment in teacher training
> colleges from the present level of
> approximately 5000 to around 21,000 by 1970.
> This should enable the annual output of
> teachers to be stepped up from 2000 a year to
> about 6000 a year by 1970. Over the course
> of the seven-year period this should result
> in the production of about 31,000 additional
> teachers, which would allow the net increase
> in the demand for teachers for the elementary
> schools to be met with trained teachers and a
> start to be made with the replacement of some
> of the pupil teachers. 37

On the university level, the plan expected that by 1970 "approximately 5,000 students will be enrolled as regular students in the three Universities..."38 with facilities provided for additional non-residential day students, making possible the expected graduation of 9000 students by 1970.39

The Seven-Year Plan is a well researched plan. The section on education is an authoritative treatise on the need for an economic approach to training, calculation of cost; efficiency in terms of deployment, and of socio-economic improvement; and budgeting for training. It recognized training for its major economic function as an investment in human capital, a function which is of the utmost importance in the industrial development of the country. The plan also weighed carefully the profitability of alternatives, timed the training periods to fit the country's development plans and aimed at an optimal deployment of the country's total resources, training to maintain vocational flexibility among the output of the educational institutions, and in making known their present and possible future output. Our only criticism of this section of the plan is that it failed to revise job descriptions so that the requirements of the pattern of manpower needs of the country will be closely satisfied by deployment of the available output of students at different levels of the educational system. It seems to us that planning rational use of manpower in a developing country, such as Ghana, would entail the following steps:

1. Better methods of recruitment to reduce waste in education.

2. Better allocation of skills among the various industrial sectors of the economy to meet manpower shortages.

3. Encouragement of on-the-job training,

4. Incentives to encourage the educated unemployed to embark on self-employment.

5. Creation of part-time employment for students.

6. Research into new avenues of employment.

7. Forecasting of manpower requirements so as to be able to plan vocational training guidance and placement activities.40

These steps are only meaningful in a developing country when the concept of education as an end in itself gives way to the concept of education as a preparation for life. The concept of education as an end in itself, unfortunately, leads to the following factos accounting for the unemployment of the educated:

1. A secondary school education which did not equip the students with any specialized skill, and thus restricted the students to the overcrowded and highly competitive clerical occupations.

2. Absence of vocational guidance services.

3. Lack of knowledge of employment opportunities, particularly in rural areas.

4. Lack of employment opportunities for educated persons in rural areas.41

To deal effectively with the problem of the educated unemployed, the government must

1. Establish a human resources center to direct the educated unemployed towards, and prepare them for, manual work and instill in them respect for manual labor;

2. Establish a production center intended to provide both training and employment and to enable the school leavers eventually to be absorbed into the regular development program.42

In almost all developing countries the problems of education, capital and management are hard to separate. Educational policies are hard to make. Some would argue for the concentration of resources more than the developing countries have tended to on high level manpower, rather than upon primary education.

Where does a developing country, such as Ghana, put its capital since its resources are limited? From a strictly technological and developmental point of view, it may well be right

for Ghana to put its capital in the industrial
sector. However, in the process of social change,
the needs of politics and citizenship challenge
the needs of industrialization. The economic need
is tempered by the need of the political, and in
this process primary education cannot be
neglected. If social change is to become a
reality, an emphasis upon primary education, with
all of the problems it creates, is vital to the
success of social change. Political leaders must
be willing to take all the risks attendant on a
heavy emphasis on primary education.

An emphasis on primary education inevitably
means that higher levels of manpower education or
skilled and technical education would be neglected
to some extent. An emphasis on primary education
creates expectations on the part of the people.
This may be good or bad. But if the people are
left in ignorance the inevitable consequence would
be that the people would become placid and
politically apathetic. There is no hope for
social change and democratic development unless
the people are brought into the whole process of
social change, and primary education, in this
respect, is the catalyst. Thomas Jefferson said
of old, in a letter to Colonel Yancey in 1816,
that

> If a nation expects to be ignorant and
> free, in a state of civilization, it expects
> what never was and never will be. The
> functionaries of every government have
> propensities to command at will the liberty
> and property of their constituents. There is
> no safe deposit for these but with the people
> themselves; nor can they be safe with them
> without information. Where the press is
> free, and every man able to read, all is
> safe.43

And to C.C. Blatchly, he wrote in 1822 on
man's happiness and popular education:

> I look to the diffusion of light and
> education as the resource most to be relied
> on for ameliorating the condition, promoting
> the virtue, and advancing the happiness of
> man. That every man shall be made virtuous,
> by any process whatever, is, indeed, no more
> to be expected than that every tree shall be
> made to bear fruit, and every plant
> nourishment. The brier and bramble can never

become the vine and olive; but their
asperities may be softened by culture, and
their properties improved to usefulness in
the order and economy of the world. And I do
hope that, in the present spirit of extending
to the great mass of mankind the blessings of
instruction, I see a prospect of great
advancement in the happiness of the human
race; and that this may proceed to an
indefinite, although not to an infinite
degree.44

One of the authorities on social change who
has dealt extensively with the educational needs
of the developing countries in terms of manpower,
neglects to some extent the issue of primary
education. Instead, he emphasizes the problem of
creating managers and supervisors—the "prime
movers of innovation." He asserts that "The
problem facing the newly developing countries,
then, is to make the high level manpower group as
innovation-conscious as possible, and to develop
within its ranks as many creative innovators as
possible."45 These prime movers with extensive
skill and knowledge must be drawn from the ranks
of the high-level manpower.46 And he includes the
following occupational categories in the
definition of high-level manpower:

1. Entrepreneurial, managerial and
   administrative personnel in both public
   and private establishments, including
   educational institutions.

2. "Qualified" teachers, defined as those
   who have had a minimum of 12 years of
   education themselves.

3. Professional personnel, such as
   scientists, engineers, architects,
   doctors, veterinarians, agronomists,
   economists, lawyers, accountants,
   journalists, artists, etc.

4. Sub-professional technical personnel,
   such as agricultural assistants,
   technicians, senior clerks, and
   supervisors of skilled workers, the
   highest level of skilled craftsmen, and
   skilled clerical workers, such as
   stenographers.

5. Top-ranking political leaders, labor
   leaders, judges, and officers of police
   and the armed forces.47

Harbison concludes that "These are the types of people who, in general, fill the strategic occupations in modern economies. From their ranks are drawn the leadership for social, political and economic activities."48 Harbison is right. But we fail to see how a developing country can create these "prime movers of innovation" without putting emphasis upon primary education, at least extricating the masses from the miasma of traditionalism and superstition. It seems to us that in a society in which the essential loyalties are primarily to kinship groups, and only in a very superficial way to the concept of the nation state, a society that is primarily non-literate, the only way that the concept of the nation state can be given solidity--and this was what Nkrumah attempted--that the processes of social change can only be accelerated through putting a major emphasis on primary education.

It must be remembered that a number of different languages are spoken in Ghana. No single language is spoken by all the people. This creates serious barriers in the modernization process. The only way to overcome these barriers is at the primary school level where all the students study English as the universal language of communication.

What Harbison proposes is the creation of a unified elite which, in many instances, have found that the only way to survive is through sloganeering, for example the attack on neo-colonialism, as a new specter of terror. This kind of sloganeering tends to hold together otherwise diverse tribal groups. In fact, this unified elite will continue to dominate the people so long as they remain ignorant. In Ghana, for instance, it was this high-level manpower group which was strongly opposed to the emergence of the kind of educational structure which would meet the needs of the country. Here we must differentiate between the political elites and the technocratic elites. The political elites are the politicians, and the technocratic elites are the fastidious opponents of changes in the educational system. Nkrumah has criticized the latter, and rightly so: he holds that they have conceived of their position as essentially one of signing papers and devotion to bureaucratic procedures, thus neglecting the fact that they are the instruments for "putting into effect the economic and social programme of the government."49

Some of the results of these educational
proposals are the establishment cf Cape Coast
University for Teacher Education, the
establishment of the Kwame Nkrumah University of
Science, Engineering and Technology at Kumasi, the
establishment of the Institutes for African
Studies and Adult Education at the University of
Ghana at Legon, and the establishment of several
secondary-technical institutes in Accra, Sekondi-
Takoradi, Kumasi, Trans-Volta Togcland Region and
the Northern Region of Ghana as well as the
establishment of agricultural institutes at Tafo,
in Ashanti Region.

Whether or not the establishment of these
institutes will have any radical impact on the
political and social development cf Ghana is yet
to be seen.

REFERENCES

1. See Eric Ashby, AFRICAN UNIVERSITIES AND
   WESTERN TRADITION (Cambridge, 1964);
   John Wilson, EDUCATION AND CHANGING WEST
   AFRICAN CULTURE (New York, 1963); L.
   Gray Cowan, et al., eds., EDUCATION AND
   NATION-BUILDING IN AFRICA (New York,
   1965).

2. Phelps-Stokes Fund, EDUCATION IN AFRICA:
   A Study of West and Equatorial Africa
   (New York, 1922), p. 16.

3. Speech at the opening cf the Institute
   of African Studies, October 25, 1963.

4. Ibid.

5. Eric Ashby, AFRICAN UNIVERSITIES, p. 20.

6. Ibid., p. 22.

7. Ibid., p. 27.

8. Ibid., p. 32.

9. Ibid., p. 41.

10. Ibid., p. 41.

11. Nkrumah, Speech at the Opening Ceremony
    of Akuafo Hall of Residence at the
    University College of the Gold Coast,
    February 17, 1956.

12. Eric Ashby, AFRICAN UNIVERSITIES, pp. 61-62.

13. GHANAIAN TIMES (October 2, 1961).

14. Nana Nketsia, quoted in GHANAIAN TIMES (January 29, 1962). There are at present (1969) three universities in Ghana.

15. UNIVERSITY OF GHANA REPORTER (October 26, 1962), p. 18.

16. "Programme for Work and Happiness" (1962), p. 36.

17. Speech delivered at a University Dinner, University of Ghana, Legon, on February 24, 1963; reprinted in the UNIVERSITY OF GHANA REPORTER (March, 1963), pp. 155-157.

18. REPORT OF THE COMMISSION CN UNIVERSITY EDUCATION, December 1960-January 1961 (Accra, 1961).

19. The government only gave the report a qualified approval. See Statement by the Government on the Report of the Commission on University Education, W.P. No.5161.

20. Kwame Nkrumah, I SPEAK OF FREEDOM, p. 167 (Party address cn the 10th anniversary of the founding of the C.P.P.).

21. Ibid., p. 167.

22. S.M. Eisenstadt, MODERNIZATION, PROTEST AND CHANGE, p. 17.

23. D.O. Mannon, PROSPERO AND CALIBAN: THE PSYCHOLOGY OF COLONIZATION (London, 1956), quoted in Ashby, AFRICAN UNIVERSITIES, p. 100.

24. GHANA: Seven-Year Development Plan, 1963-64 to 1969-70, p. 142.

25. Ibid., pp. 142-143

26. Ibid., p. 143.

27. S. Pratt and A.J. Loveridge, "Training Programs Manpower Planning", TEACHER EDUCATION, IV, 3 (London, February 1964), pp. 179-190.

28. SEVEN-YEAR PLAN, p. 143.

29. S. Pratt et. al., "Training Programs".

30. SEVEN-YEAR PLAN, p. 150.

31. Ibid., p. 150.

32. Ibid., p. 151.

33. Ibid., p. 153.

34. Ibid., p. 154.

35. Ibid., p. 156.

36. Ibid., p. 158.

37. Ibid., pp. 155-156.

38. Ibid., p. 160.

39. For the statistical projections of the plan on education, manpower and employment, refer to Appendix.

40. These steps are based on the conclusions arrived at in a study of the employment of secondary school leavers in India, published by the Government of India, Ministry of Labour and Employment, New Delhi, 1963 (Mimeographed).

41. Ibid., based on summary conclusions.

42. Ibid.

43. Quoted by Saul K. Padover in THOMAS JEFFERSON ON DEMOCRACY (New York, 1961), p. 89.

44. Ibid., p. 92.

45. Frederick Harbison, "The Prime Movers of Innovation", EDUCATION AND ECONOMIC DEVELOPMENT, edited by C. Arnold Anderson and Mary Jean Bowman (Chicago, 1965), p. 231.

46. Ibid., p. 231.

136

47. Ibid.

48. Ibid.

49. Nkrumah, AFRICA MUST UNITE, p. 88.

INDUSTRIALIZATION AND DEVELOPMENT
OF A SOCIALIST SOCIETY

In the preceding chapter we analyzed several of the problems of the developmental process in Ghana during Nkrumah's regime and Nkrumah's attempts at transforming the infrastructure of Ghanaian society. In this chapter our objective is to enumerate Nkrumah's proposals for industrialization and the development of a socialist society in Ghana.

Speaking before a seminar for senior civil servants in 1962, Nkrumah observed:

We are running against time in Africa; not only have we to eliminate or eradicate the deficiencies of our past, but we must also, in the shortest possible time, attempt to catch up with modern techniques of our time.1

And more specifically in referring to Ghana, he said:

We in Ghana are committed to the building of an industrialized socialist society. We cannot afford to sit still and be mere passive onlookers. We must ourselves take part in the pursuit of scientific and technological research as a means of providing the basis for our socialist society.2

In the post-colonial period, Nkrumah has argued, the most important objective of the nationalist elites should be a radical restructuring of the national economy and of society--an objective which he describes as "Social Reconstruction, i.e., freedom from poverty and economic exploitation and the improvement of social and economic conditions of the people so that they will be able to find better means of achieving and asserting their right to human life and happiness."3

But in order to attain this goal of social reconstruction there must come into existence an industrial economy which will replace the colonial economic structure. And as he has argued:

> Poverty is progressively reduced only as productivity increases and industrialization progresses and part of its surplus can be made available in increased wages, better housing and generally improved social conditions.4

This reconstruction of the socio-economic structures of Ghanaian society, the thesis runs, must proceed along "the socialist path" because "socialism is our only alternative".5   Three reasons have been given by Nkrumah as to why socialism is the only alternative: Firstly, for a developing country, such as Ghana, to follow the capitalist way of development would mean that control of the national economy would remain in the hands of private foreign capital. This would lead to a neo-colonialist regime in Ghana because "colonial rule precluded that accumulation of capital among our citizens which would have assisted thorough-going private investment in industrial construction."6   Secondly, the publicly-owned enterprises "capitalized out of national funds" by the colonial government, such as the railways, harbors and electric power must continue to be publicly owned and run by the state, for to transfer these enterprises to private interest would be to betray "the trust of the great masses of our people to the greedy interests of a small coterie of individuals, probably in alliance with foreign capitalists."7 Thirdly, the "production for private profit deprives a large section of the people of the goods and services produced."8 For these reasons, Nkrumah has postulated that economic reconstruction and technological and social change in Ghana must follow the path of socialism.

In the process of economic reconstruction and technological and social change, Nkrumah sets forth ten basic principles which, if adhered to, would transform the infrastructure of Ghanaian society. But in this process a sort of development ideology must be evolved--and as the editors of The Spark put it, "a 'non-ideological' approach to economic development leads to confusion and the strengthening of externally directed capitalism."9   It is this ideological approach to economic development and technological and social change that determined the ten basic principles for social transformation that Nkrumah postulated.

According to Nkrumah, there are three stages in the modernization process. The first stage is the period of socio-economic reconstruction when the government concentrates on improving educational and health facilities and expanding the communications media--i.e., the infrastructure for economic growth. The second stage is characterized by the government's determination to achieve economic independence; and this prepares the ground for the third stage, a socialist society. In the transitional period before a socialist society becomes a reality, the ten basic principles underlying the process must be scrupulously taken into account. These principles have been fully discussed in his book, Africa Must Unite, to which all further references are made.

First principle: the state must play the major role in economic development. "Because colonialism prevented the emergence of a strong local capitalist class, because production for private profit is based on exploitation, and because the less developed nations need a high rate of economic growth, the government is obliged to play the role of main entrepreneur in laying the basis of national economic and social advancement."10 There are, however, other factors influencing the approach to economic development, i.e., the need to break away from "the European monopoly domination of our economy", which thus creates the necessity for the government to be "extremely vigilant in scenting out the subtle and insidious infiltrations of neo-colonialism", and the ever-present danger of sabotage by foreigners enjoying...the privilege of building economic enterprises in our midst."11 Given these considerations, Nkrumah has concluded that "the government has to take the place of the adventurous entrepreneurs who created the capital basis of industrialization in the advanced countries."12

Second principle: national economic planning must be the principal lever for the total development of society. National economic planning must reflect "the strictest control to safeguard against unrelated overspending on any project", but, however, "there must be a certain elasticity to allow for emendation or adjustment without upsetting the general plan and our budgeting". Planning must also seek to control reinvestment measures on profit made by foreign and local concerns. "Government interference in all matters affecting economic growth in less developed countries", Nkrumah argues, "is today a universally accepted principle, and interests, domestic or foreign, enjoying the opportunities of profitable gain, cannot object to some control of the reinvestment of part of that gain in the national development of the country in which it is reaped."13 Another aspect of national economic planning Nkrumah called for, is greater participation by the state in economic activities. He opined that "Our planning will be geared to our policy of increasing governmental participation in the nation's economic activities, and all enterprises are expected to accept this policy..."14

Third principle: national planning for economic development and social transformation of society must be geared to socialism. To attain this socialist goal, Nkrumah elucidated nine factors as constituting the core of the process:

1. A Mixed Economy: under a mixed economy, the economic system must be divided into several sectors with the state exercising overall control of the activities of the various sectors. Under Nkrumah, there were five sectors--state enterprises; privately owned foreign enterprises; joint enterprises owned by the state and foreign private interests; cooperatives; and enterprises exclusively reserved for Ghanaian entrepreneurs. The crux here is that each sector operated within limits established by the state. The limits were such that there was considerable room for the state sectors to expand at the expense of the private sectors of the economy. This was in keeping with Nkrumah's design to build a socialist society. To allow the private sectors to expand at the expense of the state sectors would be to allow the development of capitalism and capitalist infrastructure of society.15

2. New economic institutions must be developed to replace the colonial economic institutions. To continue to use the old colonial economic institutions, dependent upon a one-crop economy, in the post-colonial period would be to maintain and increase the dominant role of the colonial master, which inevitably could lead to neo-colonialism--the essence of which "is that the state which is subject to it is, in theory, independent and has all the outward trappings of international sovereignty. In reality, its

economic system and, thus, its political policy is
directed from outside."16

3. Revolutionizing of agriculture, i.e.,
the introduction of modern techniques of farming
to increase agricultural productivity. The
objective of this is to meet the "needs of the
domestic market" and "to provide raw materials for
secondary industries". The attainment of this
objective requires experimental plantations of new
crops, experimental agricultural centers for the
application of new techniques to farming. In the
last resort, what is also required is a mental
adjustment of the farm population to the ever
increasing demands of technology. They must be
jolted out of their religious and magical
acceptance of life and traditional ways of farming
into accepting modern equipment for farming. This
task requires an educational program which will
deal practically with the burning problems of
traditional attitudes toward farming.

4. The state itself must be the main source
to provide capital for development. To provide
capital, "surpluses must be pressed out of rising
production to finance development" and the
population must "forego some immediate personal
desire for a greater benefit a bit later on."17
What rankles most in this approach is the fear of
economic exploitation and the dominant role of the
colonial master in the economic sphere. Hence the
need to become economically independent of foreign
private capital and influence.

5. The state must guarantee a basic minimum
standard of living for all. To achieve this basic
minimum standard, "prices of goods should not
exceed wages; house rentals must be within the
means of all groups; social welfare services must
be open to all; educational and cultural amenities
must be available to everyone."18 But purely
social services at the expense of other increased
amenities to the people are rejected on the
grounds that: "The welfare state is the climax of
a highly developed industrialism. To assure its
benefits in a less developed country is to promise
merely the division of poverty."19

6. Training of manpower. There is, first
of all, the point that in a developing country
long-term planning in all sections of life and,
therewith, unavoidable decisions fitted to the
frame of a policy of social and political change,
are obviously much more urgent. To the extent to
which the political leadership of the country

grasps the need that human life must be planned
instead of being left to chance, it would be led
back to the question of responsibility of leading
the struggle for social and political change.20

7. Industrial and technological planning
must encourage the creation of plants in which "we
have a natural advantage in local resources and
labour or where we can produce essential
commodities required for development or for
domestic consumption."21

8. The investment policy of the country
must provide the atmosphere for the growth of
local industries. Investment priority must be
determined by the rate of capital formation,
savings on imported goods, boom on exported goods,
and a reduction in the development gap between the
different sections of the country to prevent the
urban centers from becoming overcrowded.

9. "Active participation of the people
through their own organization in the process of
economic planning and development."22 It is this
point that raises the most difficult questions of
political and social transformation to which we
have already paid some attention. The
participation of the people though essential to
democracy is not necessary for the people to have
"the control of the means of production and
distribution", as Nkrumah seems to argue.23

Fourth Principle: foreign capital must be
welcomed, but in a manner that will not compromise
the integrity and sovereignty of the country.
"Foreign capital is thus useful and helpful if it
takes the form of a loan or credit to enable the
borrowing country to buy what it needs from
whatever sources it likes, and at the same time to
retain control of the assets to be developed."24

This principle is the characteristic trait of
a developing country and is manifested strongly in
the political sphere. The first reaction of a
country in the post-colonial phase is, by and
large, a conscious revulsion from its former
relations with the colonial master. This is
partly dictated by requirements of domestic policy
and propaganda. It is only slowly that the
realization dawns that collaboration with the
erstwhile colonial master can be fruitful and that
the offer of help from the Soviet bloc countries
must not be accepted without due consideration.
And it is the dichotomy between the West and the

Soviet bloc countries, at least on the political level, that enables the developing countries to adopt a neutralist attitude, i.e., a position midway between the East and the West. Thus, in the process of seeking foreign capital, the attempt is to seek terms that will "preserve integrity and sovereignty without crippling economic or political ties to any country, bloc or system."25

Fifth Principle: the diversification of foreign economic links. "This enables a country to avoid the dangers of 'crippling ties to any one country' and helps in the drive for stable and better prices for our primary commodities on the world's markets. It must be pointed out that 'stable and high' world prices for our products will increase the surpluses that could be ploughed into industrialization. It will also put economic planning on a firmer footing."26

Sixth Principle: some of the social attitudes of the people must change if there is to occur a social and political transformation of society. "The drag on economic activity of the extended family ssystem, and the habit of squandering large sums of money on social festivities"27 must be brought to an end, and replaced by a "new spirit of hard work, and savings for production..."28 The most difficult problem is how to break away from the old traditional beliefs that are no longer adequate for a technological and industrialized society. The difficulty, however, was to find some means of accommodating the old traditional and cultural beliefs to modern ways of life. Nkrumah proposed a radical solution--"Our less energetic society must be goaded into the acceptance of the stimuli necessary to rapid economic development by alterations in our social relationships and habits if necessary by law."29

This kind of radical approach does not take into account that Ghana as a nation is made up of manifold ethnological parts or several tribal groups, that it does not have a common language through which a unified consciousness might be created to replace the plethora of local and tribal loyalties, and that Ghana, as a nation, is simply the result of historical delimitation. Experience, so far, has shown that law by itself is not an agent for the radicalization of socio-political consciousness.

Seventh Principle: the rise of a bourgeois class must be prevented. Particular attention was

directed to the intelligentsia and the political
elite. Nkrumah was particularly concerned that
the emergence of a privileged class in the post-
colonial period would undermine his socialist
programs. Thus he directed all of his attention
to crushing any signs of class consciousness or
class solidarity on the part of the intelligentsia
and the business community. He was thus forced to
take a stand against the appearance of the
emergence of a privileged political class in his
"Dawn Broadcast" of April 8, 1961. "I spoke of
the dangers arising from Ghanaian public men
attempting to combine business with political
life, and warned that those who could not give
entirely disinterested service should leave
politics or be thrown out. Legislation has since
limited the amount of property our public men may
own."30 It was merely a speech aimed at pacifying
the people. The various commissions established
after the military coup to investigate the
activities of the members of the C.P.P. have well
documented the fact that the activists of the
C.P.P. were, at the same time, the privileged
class in the society. This contradiction in
theory and practice was well known to critical
observers of Nkrumah long before the military
take-over.

Eighth Principle: a new budgetary and fiscal
structure must be developed totally different from
the colonial budgetary and fiscal structure. "The
criteria of this new system must be a release of
initiative for economic production the husbanding
of national financial resources, the efficient and
effective direction of investment for national
development, and the prevention of the flight of
capital away from the country...In the performance
of these tasks, the new fiscal system will use the
State budget, import control, the State bank and
an investment bank as its principal weapons."31

Ninth Principle: the Convention People's
Party must be the vanguard of the people leading
the struggle for socialism and must play a
strategic role in the economic development and
social and political transformation of the
country.32

Tenth Principle: the administrative
machinery of the country must constantly undergo
change because the country is in a state of flux.
Since the administrative officials are charged
with administering the affairs of the country and
being the administrative arm of the government,

they must perform the tasks which are entrusted to them by the political party in power.33   And, as if to intimidate the civil servants, Nkrumah stated: "I am averse to our civil servants being lodged in the state apparatus like a nail without a head: once you drive it in you cannot pull it out.   Government   must   retain   the   right   of dismissal, and the civil servant must be   made   to realize that he can be dismissed if he does not perform the job required of him.   He must be grappling with his work all the time, thinking twenty-four hours a day how best he can serve   his country."34

In analyzing the programs of Nkrumah and the C.P.P. the essential thing to be taken into account is his conception of Marxism as a guide to social action,   societal   change,   and industrial development.   This, we believe, is the key to understanding the actions of Nkrumah.

While studying law at the London School of Economics   in   1947,   he made   known   his interpretation   of   imperialism and devised a strategy for decolonialization.   In his Towards Colonial Freedom; Africa in the Struggle Against World Imperialism, he literally applied the Marxist-Leninist interpretation of imperialism to Africa.   In this monograph, he echoed Lenin's conceptions   about   "colonialism   as   monopoly financed capitalism", "the uneven development of capitalism",   "the inevitability of war under imperialism",   the   radicalization   of   class consciousness of the working people, and the desirability of forming an alliance between the peoples of the colony and the working class of the capitalist countries of the West.   The monograph was meant to initiate the "organization of the colonial masses" for independence.   In it, Nkrumah opined that "the goal of the national liberation movement is the realization of complete and unconditional independence, and the building of a society of peoples in which the   free   development of each is the condition for the free development of all."35

Despite Marxist-Leninist themes, which recur in Nkrumah's works and speeches, economically he moved toward the acceptance of a mixed economy rather than complete ownership by the state.   The Marxist-Leninist themes remain mainly on the level of humanistic aspirations.   For Nkrumah,   the essence of socialism is equal opportunity for all; the withering away of individual and class exploitation;   and a system of economic production

beneficial to the totality of society rather than
to individuals and groups.36 In theory, socialism
meant distributive justice; and, in practice, the
means of attaining this end is a mixed economy.

In the Seven-Year Development Plan, the Ghana
government aimed for a balance between the private
and public sectors of the economy. The government
provided for five sectors operating within the
economy: inter alia, (1) the government and
private foreign investors would enter into
partnership in jointly owned state-private
enterprises.37 The government, in anticipation of
this partnership, banned all enterprises jointly
owned by individual Ghanaians and foreign
investors; (2) Ghanaian citizens under the plan
would have had exclusive control of the small-
scale private enterprise sector; foreign investors
would have had control over larger economic
enterprises. This approach to economics deviates
from the originally universalistic Marxian
approach to socialism.

A careful analysis of Nkrumah's writings,
speeches and programs all indicates that he did
not develop any elaborate systematic economic
theory. Instead he followed a pragmatic economic
program independent of both capitalism and the
communist model.

In the political and philosophical thought of
Nkrumah, there recurs the concept of social
equilibrium and humanism--that a socialist Ghana
should aspire to secure a balance of human and
societal needs, an equilibrium between
materialistic values and socio-cultural and
spiritual values--because in traditional African
society there already existed a harmonious
relation between the materialistic and the
spiritual, the interest of the individual and the
general interest of society as a whole. Thus it
is the sacred duty of government to preserve an
equilibrium between the private and public sectors
of the economy and between the industrial and
agricultural sectors of society; and to uphold
humanism in all things because, in the words of
Senghor, the poet-president of Senegal, "Negro
African society is collectivist, or, more exactly,
communal because it is rather a communion of souls
than an aggregate of individuals...We had already
realized socialism before the coming of the
European...Our duty is to renew it by helping it
to regain spiritual dimensions."38

These are some of the principles which Nkrumah argued will guide the political leadership in the process of industrialization and the development of a socialist society in Ghana. But was Nkrumah able to translate these principles into action? If not, then why? Any assessment of Nkrumah's attempts to transform Gharaian society must take into consideration his commitment to Pan-Africanism. It may very well be argued that his commitment to Pan-Africanism and his fervent interest in African interstate unity, and his belief in the supreme efficacy of politics may have abetted his attempts to industrialize Ghana and to transform it into a socialist society.

REFERENCES

1.   Speech at the Seminar for Senior Civil Servants at Winneba, April 14, 1962.

2.   Speech at the laying of the foundation stone of the atomic reactor at Kwabenya, November 25, 1964.

3.   Nkrumah, TOWARDS COLONIAL FREEDOM, p. 43.

4.   NKrumah, AFRICA MUST UNITE, p. 106.

5.   Ibid., p. 119.

6.   Ibid.

7.   Ibid.

8.   Ibid.

9.   Some Essential Features of NKRUMAISM, p. 54.

10.   Ibid., p. 119.

11.   Ibid., p. 102.

12.   Ibid., p. 110.

13.   Ibid., p. 120.

14.   Ibid., p. 120.

15.   Ibid., See p. 123 for a discussion of national planning and the development of socialism.

16. Nkrumah, NEC-COLONIALISM, p. ix.

17. Nkrumah, AFRICA MUST UNITE, p. 123.

18. Ibid., p. 119.

19. Ibid., p. 105.

20. See UNO "International Survey of Programs of Social Development" (New York, 1959), p. 7, for a discussion of social change and political leadership.

21. NKRUMAH, AFRICA MUST UNITE, p. 111.

22. SCME ESSENTIAL FEATURES OF NKRUMAISM, p. 62.

23. Nkrumah, AFRICA MUST UNITE, p. 129.

24. Ibid., p. 101.

25. Ibid., p. 102.

26. Eds. of THE SPARK, NKRUMAISM, pp. 64-65.

27. Ibid., p. 65.

28. Ibid.

29. Nkrumah, AFRICA MUST UNITE, p. 105.

30. Ibid., p. 124.

31. Eds. of THE SPARK, NKRUMAISM, pp. 66-67.

32. See Section (a) "The Role of the Party as Agent of Social Change" for a full discussion. Supra, p. 122.

33. Nkrumah, AFRICA MUST UNITE, p. 88.

34. Ibid., p. 93.

35. Nkrumah, TOWARDS COLCNIAL FREEDOM, p. 43.

36. See GUIDE TO PARTY ACTION, p. 6.

37. See PROGRAM OF THE C.P.P. FOR WORK AND
     HAPPINESS.

38. L. Senghor, AFRICAN SOCIALISM, p. 32,
     cited in C.F. Andrian, "Democracy and
     Socialism", IDEOLOGY AND DISCONTENT,
     David E. Apter, ed. (Glencoe, 1964), p.
     178.

The struggle against imperialism which erupted in West Africa after World War II was initiated in Europe. It was at the Pan-African Congresses that the strategy for the decolonization process in Africa was mapped. At these Congresses Africans from British and French territories quoted the Atlantic Charter and the Four Freedoms as their mandate for the struggle against imperialism.

From the early beginnings of imperialism in West Africa, there had been nationalist leaders and movements. The Aborigines' Rights Protection Society in the Gold Coast was founded in 1897 to protect the lands of the chiefs and people of the Gold Coast. The National Congress of British West Africa emerged in 1920 under the leadership of J.E. Casely-Hayford of the Gold Coast. The NCBWA aimed at some form of federation of the four British West African Colonies, i.e., Gambia, the Gold Coast, Nigeria and Sierra Leone. A decade later, the NCBWA was followed by a more radical youth movement, the West African Youth League.

But it was not until 1947, when Dr. J.B. Danquah brought the politically conscious lawyers in the Gold coast to form the United Gold Coast Convention, "to ensure by all legitimate and constitutional means the direction and control of government should pass into the hands of the people and their chiefs" that a more serious attempt was made to challenge imperialism. But, the aim of these lawyers and chiefs was simply to replace the colonial officials by black men, and not to change the structure of society as it had developed under the traditional rulers and the British.

Meanwhile, an increasing number of the younger generation had begun to express protest not only against colonialism but against traditional authorities and African-exploiting merchants.

By the beginning of 1948 many felt that some kind of change was bound to come. But, what form it would take depended on the outcome of two conflicts within the nationalist camp. The nationalists were all against colonialism. But within their ranks there was another struggle between the younger generation and the old leaders for control of the nationalist movement. This struggle eventually led to the breakaway of the younger generation from the U.G.C.C. and the formation of the Convention People's Party under the leadership of Kwame Nkrumah.

The real "revolutionary" period in the political history of the Gold Coast opened on December 16, 1947, with the arrival of Kwame Nkrumah from Britain. He had been invited, on the recommendation of a former classmate at Lincoln University, to return home and become secretary of the U.G.C.C. Nkrumah's education in the United States and Britain, in addition to his contacts with socialist political groups in America and Britain, had given him a grounding in political strategy which was to prove the decisive influence in the political history of the Gold Coast.

Until Nkrumah's arrival in the Gold Coast, political agitation had been largely confined to efforts by Dr. J.B. Danquah and the chiefs and a few lawyers to extricate themselves from colonialism and to replace colonial rule with their own. Nkrumah, on the other hand, was to lead a political "revolution" whose aim was to bring about a profound social change.

Nkrumah's central political tactic was to use every grievance to point to the political and moral issues involved in the struggle and to seize political advantage. Here, then, was the first, pragmatic and programatic political platform on which Nkrumah and the C.P.P. were to canvass nationally for national support. Nkrumah attacked colonialism and the U.G.C.C. simultaneously; traditional authorities were shown to be holding on to their power and retarding the progress of the people in defiance of their just aspirations. The colonial power was accused of offering a superficially meaningless representative system of government whilst retaining the essentials of power through the Governor and the colonial officials.

The formation of the C.P.P. was related to one overriding objective --the political independence of Ghana. The C.P.P. would eventually lead Ghana to independence in 1957. After independence, the opportunity presented itself for a major advance towards socio-economic and political development. Opinions differed somewhat in Ghana and within the C.P.P. as to the

preferred route to social change and political
development, but there was general agreement
(especially within the C.P.P.) that political
freedom, national planning and economic
development were closely linked.

Within the ranks of Nkrumah's opponents there
was a leaning towards gradualism, while the
leaders of the C.P.P. regarded political
independence as a necessary first step to rapid
social change and economic development. The
C.P.P. regarded political independence as a means
of effecting fundamental changes in Ghanaian
society.

It was Kwame Nkrumah as the Life-Chairman of
the C.P.P. who constructed a forceful and an
articulate developmental ideology describing the
aspirations of the Ghanaians. Stressing the close
relationship between theory and practice, and
between political ideology and economic
development, Nkrumah pointed out how political
independence presented Ghanaians the opportunity
to fundamentally alter the structure of their
society and to alter the pattern of traditional
agriculture, to create a corps of technicians
capable of operating the mechanics of an evolving
industrial society, and to develop new social
values consonant with an egalitarian social
system. This radical transformation of society,
he argued, would require a high degree of state
control and a rigorous state authority in all
spheres of life; hence there had to be an
effectively centralized government and an end to
such divisive institutions as tribalism,
regionalism and the two-party system.

The central authority and the C.P.P. would
organize the rural areas, not through the chiefly
institutions or some form of regionalism, but
through a network of local political councils and
party activists responsible to the central
authority. In order to ensure the continued
effectiveness of the state, Nkrumah opined,
democratic processes would be honored, but
traditionalist and separatist political opposition
and the luxury of democracy would have to give way
to some form of authoritarianism.

Outdated socio-economic institutions in Ghana
would have to change, Nkrumah argued. The
extended family system which encouraged nepotism
and a system of gifts and bribes, and rewarded
indolence, retarded productivity, prevented

savings and discriminated against the energetic
and resourceful, would all have to go. Polygamy
was an impediment, as were laws of succession and
inheritance designed to stifle the creative urge;
they would all have to go. Customs regulating
stool lands and landholding would have to be
revised to strengthen titles and enable the owners
to raise capital and to finance commerce and light
industry. A desire for planned saving, long
discouraged under traditional patterns of extended
family responsibility, would have to be instilled
in the interests of capital formation. Corruption
and bribery in government were to be replaced by
an integrity in public life equal to the task of
national reconstruction.

One of the basic reasons of the attack on
traditionalism, Nkrumah argued, was the necessity
for effecting a revolution in agriculture
production. Agricultural productivity had to be
raised and changed from a purely subsistence level
to cultivation carefully designed to provide
adequate food for a rising population while
supplying local industries with raw materials and
producing cash crops which could pay for necessary
industrial imports.

Nevertheless, Nkrumah argued, a revolution in
agricultural production was insufficient without
complementary industrialization. To finance
industrialization foreign investment would be
needed, but Nkrumah argued that the state should
assume as great a share of the investment burden
as possible in order to forestall attempts by
foreign investors striving to gain control of the
country's resources.

For Nkrumah, political independence was the
first step towards modernization. "Seek ye first
the political kingdom". This parody of Christ's
injunction became the foundation of much of
Nkrumah's strategy. The positive and articulate
program of the C.P.P. on Work and Happiness and
the Seven Year Plan of the government, enunciated
by an attractive and energetic leader, the first
to engineer political independence in West Africa,
had strong appeal to other Africans under colonial
domination and captured the imagination of foreign
observers as well. Unhappily, though, Nkrumah
emerged in time, not as an architect of societal
change in Ghana, but as an idealist corrupted by
delusions of grandeur and infallibility, not as a
pragmatist capable of giving stability to the new
political independence of Ghana, but as a

revolutionary romantic who confused his personal
judgment with absolute truth and his self-esteem
with universal public approval. The result was a
steady deterioration of Ghana's political and
economic situation. The national economy of Ghana
was brought to a point of bankruptcy by a
combination of a policy of Pan-Africanism and
excessive zeal for industrialization.
Preoccupation with the dangers of political
opposition led to a one-party state with Nkrumah
leading a party and a government increasingly
isolated from the people, increasingly corrupt and
inefficient. When Nkrumah and his government and
the C.P.P. fell from power in February, 1966, his
overthrow delineated with awful clarity the gap
that had developed between the ideals he had
expressed so forcefully and convincingly and the
reality of his failure.

1. Theoretical Framework

THE SOCIOLOGICAL PERSPECTIVE:

Abel, Theodore, "The Present Status of Social Theory". AMERICAN SOCIOLOGICAL REVIEW, 17 (April, 1952), pp. 156-164.

Blumer, Herbert. "What is Wrong With Social Theory?" American Sociological Review, 19 (February, 1954), pp. 3-10.

Dahrendorf, Ralf. "Out of Utopia: Towards a Reorientation of Sociological Analysis". AMERICAN JOURNAL OF SOCIOLOGY, 64 (September, 1958), pp. 115-127.

Freund, Julien. THE SOCIOLOGY OF MAX WEBER (New York, Pantheon Books, Random House, Inc., 1968).

Mills, C. Wright. THE SOCIOLOGICAL IMAGINATION. New York, Oxford University Press, 1959.

"Sociological Theory and Contemporary Politics". AMERICAN JOURNAL OF SOCIOLOGY, 63 (September, 1955), pp. 105-115.

Parsons, Talcott. THE SOCIAL SYSTEM. Glencoe, The Free Press of Glencoe, 1944.

Parsons, Talcott, and Shils, Edward A. Eds. TOWARD A GENERAL THEORY OF ACTION. New York, Harper & Row, Publishers, 1965.

Wrong, Dennis H. "The Oversocialized Conception of Man in Modern Sociology". AMERICAN SOCIOLOGICAL REVIEW 26 (April, 1961) pp. 183-193.

THE MARXIST LEVEL:

Coser, Lewis. THE FUNCTIONS OF SOCIAL CONFLICT. New York, The Free Press, 1956.

Dahrendorf, Ralf. CLASS AND CLASS CONFLICT IN INDUSTRIAL SOCIETY. Stanford, Stanford University Press, 1959.

Dahrendorf, Ralf. "Towards a Theory of Social Conflict". THE JOURNAL OF CONFLICT RESOLUTION. Vol. VII, No. 2 (June, 1958), pp. 170-183.

Simmel, George. CONFLICT AND THE WEB OF GROUP-AFFILIATIONS. New York, The Free Press, 1955.

THE POLITICAL PERSPECTIVES:

Almond, Gabriel A. and James Coleman. THE POLITICS OF THE DEVELOPING AREAS. Princeton, Princeton University Press, 1960.

Apter, David. THE POLITICS OF MODERNIZATION. Chicago, The University of Chicago Press, 1965.

Deutsch, K.W. NATIONALISM AND SOCIAL COMMUNICATION, Mass., M.I.T. Press, 1953.

"Social Mobilization and Political Development." AMERICAN POLITICAL SCIENCE REVIEW, XLIV, 3 (September, 1961).

Deutsch, K.W. and W.J. Folz, eds. NATION-BUILDING. New York, Atherton Press, 1966.

Emerson, Rupert. FROM EMPIRE TO NATION. Boston, Beacon Press, 1964.

Kautsky, John H. POLITICAL CHANGE IN UNDERDEVELOPED COUNTRIES: NATIONALISM AND COMMUNISM. New York, John Wiley & Sons, Inc., 1962.

Lenin, V.I. STATE AND REVOLUTION. New York, International Publishers, 1932.

Lipsett, S.M. POLITICAL MAN: THE SOCIAL BASES OF POLITICS. Garden City, N.Y., Doubleday & Company, Inc., 1960.

Michels, R. POLITICAL PARTIES. New York, Collier Books, 1962.

Mills, C.W. THE POWER ELITE. New York, Oxford University Press, 1959.

Mosca, G. THE RULING CLASS. New York, McGraw-Hill, 1939.

Pye, L.W. ASPECTS OF POLITICAL DEVELOPMENT. Boston & Toronto, Little, Brown & Company, 1966.

POLITICS, PERSONALITY, AND NATION-BUILDING. New Haven, Yale University Press, 1962.

Sorel, G. REFLECTIONS ON VIOLENCE, New York, Collier Books 1961.

Wriggins, Howard. "Impediments to Unity in New Nationa". AMERICAN POLITICAL SCIENCE REVIEW, XLIV, 2 (June, 1961).
                    II. On Ghana

SUBSTANTIVE AND SECONDARY WORKS:

"Accountant-General's Department Report and Financial Statements by the Accountant General and Report Thereon by the Auditor-General 1959/60". Accra: Government Printer, 1960.

Anderson, C.A., and M.J. Bowman. EDUCATION AND ECONOMIC DEVELOPMENT. Chicago: Aldine Publishing Company, 1963.

Apter, David E. GHANA IN TRANSITION. New York: Atheneum, 1963.

"Nkrumah, Charisma, and the Coup". DEADALUS, (Summer, 1968), pp. 757-792.

"The Role of Traditionalism in the Political Modernization of Ghana and Uganda". WORLD POLITICS, XII (October, 1960), pp. 45-68.

Ashby, Eric. AFRICAN UNIVERSITIES AND WESTERN TRADITION. Cambridge: Harvard University Press, 1964.

UNIVERSITIES: BRITISH, INDIAN, AFRICAN. Cambridge: Harvard University Press, 1966.

Birch, Lionel. GHANA IS BORN, 6TH MARCH 1957. London: N. Neame, 1958.

Bloch, Henry Simon. "A Programme for Technical Assistance in the Fiscal and Financial

FRANCIS A. BOTCHWAY

Field". Prepared for the Government of
Ghana. New York: United Nations
Technical Assistance Programme, 1958.

Busia, Kofi Abrefa. AFRICA IN SEARCH OF
DEMOCRACY. New York: Praeger, 1967.

THE CHALLENGE OF AFRICA. New York:
Praeger, 1964.

Busia, Kofi Abrefa. THE POSITION OF THE CHIEF IN
THE MODERN POLITICAL SYSTEM OF ASHANTI.
A study of the influence of contemporary
social changes on Ashanti political
institutions. London: Oxford University
Press for the International African
Institute, 1951.

PURPOSEFUL EDUCATION FOR AFRICA. The
Hague, Mouton, 1964 (Publication of the
Institute of Social Studies, Series
Minor, v. 4).

REPORT ON A SOCIAL SURVEY OF SEKONDI-
TAKORADI. London: Crown Agents for the
Colonies on behalf of the Government of
the Gold Coast, 1950.

U.S. Congress. Senate. Committee of the
Judiciary. "Is I.S. Money Aiding
Another Communist State?" Hearing
before the subcommittee to investigate
the Administration of the Internal
Security Laws of the Committee on the
Judiciary, United States Senate, Eighty-
Seventh Congress, Second Session.
Testimony of K. A. Busia, December 3,
1962. Washington, U.S. Government
Printing Office, 1963.

"Education and Social Mobility in
Economically Underdeveloped Countries".
Transactions of the Third World Congress
of Sociology. Vol. V (London:
International Sociological Association,
1956), pp. 81-89.

Cowan, L., Gray, et al. EDUCATION AND NATION-
BUILDING IN AFRICA. New York: F.A.
Praeger, 1965.

Dei-Anang, Michael. GHANA RESURGENT. Accra:
Waterville Publishing Home, 1964.

"Exchange of Notes between the Governments of Ghana and Togo". Accra: Government Printing Department, 1962 (Confidential).

"Ghana". Commission of Enquiry into the Working and Administration of the Present Company Law of Ghana-Final Report". Accra: Government Printer, 1961.

"Ghana. Commission on University Education. Report of the Commission on University Education." December 1960-January 1961. Accra: Ministry of Information, 1961.

"Ghana. Constituent Assembly, 1960: Proceedings of the Constituent Assembly". 14th March to 29th June, 1960. Official Report. Accra: Government Printer, 1960.

"Ghana. Government Proposals for a Republican Constitution". Accra: Government Printer, 1960.

"Ghana. Hearing by the Judicial Committee of the Privy Council of Appeals from Courts or Judges in Ghana; exchange of letters between the Government of the United Kingdom and the Government of Ghana." London: H.M. Stationary Office, 1960.

"Ghana. Seven-Year Development Plan 1963/64 to 1969/70". Accra: Ghana, 1963.

"Ghana. Statements by the Government on the Report of the Commission on University Education, December 1960-January 1961". Accra: Ministry of Information, 1961.

Harvey, William Burnett. LAW AND SOCIAL CHANGE IN GHANA. Princeton N.J.: Princeton University Press, 1966.

Hayford, Joseph Ephraim Casely. GOLD COAST NATIVE INSTITUTIONS. With thoughts upon a Healthy Imperial Policy for the Gold Coast and Ashanti. London: Sweet & Maxwell, Ltd., 1903.

In the High Court (Special Criminal Division). The State versus Robert Benjamin Otchere, Joseph Yaw Manu, Tamia Adamafio, Ako Adjei, Hugh Horatio Cofie,

Crabbe (Judgment of the Court, 9th December, 1963). Accra, Ghana, 1963.

Kilson, M.L. "African Political Change and the Modernization Process." JOURNAL OF MODERN AFRICAN STUDIES, I (1963), pp. 435-440.

"Nationalism and Social Classes in British West Africa". The Journal of Politics, XX 91958), pp. 368-387.

Kuper, Hilda, ed. Urbanization and Migration in West Africa. Berkeley: University of California Press, 1965.

Little, Kenneth L. WEST AFRICAN URBANIZATION. London: Cambridge University Press, 1965.

Mercier, P. "Problems in Social Stratification in West Africa". CAHIERS INTERNATIONAUX DE SOCIOLOGIE, XVII (1954), pp. 47-65.

Nkrumah, Kwame. AFRICA MUST UNITE. New York: F.A. Praeger, 1963.

"1960 Ghana Population Census". Accra: Ministry of Information and Broadcasting on behalf of the Central Bureau of Statistics, 1962-1964.

Nkrumah, Kwame. THE AUTOBIOGRAPHY OF KWAME NKRUMAH. Edinburgh: T. Nelson, 1957.

AXIOMS OF KWAME (NKRUMAH). London: Nelson, 1967.

CHALLENGE OF THE CONGO. New York: International Publishers, 1967.

CONSCIENCISM. New York: Monthly Review Press, 1965.

DARK DAYS IN GHANA. New York: International Publishers, 1968.

"Death of Patrice Lumumba: A Series of Speeches, Statements and Comments by Osagyefo Dr. K. Nkrumah, between February 14 and February 20, 1961." Accra, Ghana, 1960.

HANDS OFF AFRICA!!! Some Famous
Speeches. With a Tribute to George
Padmore written by Tawia Adamafio.
Accra: Kwabena Ousufu-Akyem, 1960.

I SPEAK OF FREEDOM: A Statement of
African Ideology. New York: Praeger,
1961.

NEO-COLONIALISM: The Last Stage of
Imperialism. London: Nelson, 1965.

TOWARDS COLONIAL FREEDOM: Africa in the
Struggle Against World Imperialism.
London: Heineman, 1962.

"The Nkrumaist". Winneba, Kwame Nkrumah
Ideological Institute. Accra: 1961.

Phillips, John Frederick Vicars. KWAME NKRUMAH
AND THE FUTURE OF AFRICA. New York:
Praeger, 1961.

Ruben, Leslie and Pauli Murray. THE CONSTITUTION
AND GOVERNMENT OF GHANA. London: Sweet
& Maxwell, 1961.

SECOND DEVELOPMENT PLAN, 1959-64. Accra:
Government Printer. 1959.

Spark, The, Editors of SOME ESSENTIAL FEATURES OF
NKRUMAISM. New York: International
Publishers, 1965.

"Statement by the Government on the Recent
Conspiracy". Monday, 11 December 1961.
Accra: Ministry of Information and
Broadcasting.

"Statement by the Government on the Report of the
Commission Appointed to Enquire into the
Matters Disclosed at the Trial of
Captain Benjamin Acolientey Before a
Court-Martial, and the Surrounding
Circumstances". Accra: Government
Printer, 1959.

"Statement by the Government on the Report of the
Commission on University Education,
December 1960-January, 1961". Accra:
Ministry of Information, printed by
Government Printing Office, 1961.

"Survey of High Level Manpower in Ghana, 1960".
Accra: Ministry of Information, 1962.

162

Timothy, Bankole. KWAME NKRUMAH: HIS RISE TO
        POWER. Forword by Kojo Botsio (2nd
        Edition). Evanston, Ill.: Northwestern
        University Press, 1963.

"White   Paper   on   Marriage,   Divorce   and
        Inheritance",   Accra: Government
        Printer, 1961.

Wilson, John. EDUCATION AND CHANGING WEST AFRICAN
        CULTURE. New York: Columbia University
        Press, 1963.

SOME GENERAL THEORETICAL WORKS ON SOCIAL CHANGE:

Allen, Francis R. TECHNOLOGY AND SOCIAL CHANGE.
        New   York: Appleton-Century-Crofts,
        1957.

Aron, Raymond. THE INDUSTRIAL SOCIETY: Three
        Essays on Ideology and Development. New
        York: Praeger, 1967.

Barnett, Homer G. INNOVATION: THE BASIS OF
        CULTURAL CHANGE. 1st edition. New
        York: McGraw-Hill, 1953.

Bennis, Warren G. et al., eds. THE PLANNING OF
        CHANGE: READINGS IN APPLIED BEHAVIORAL
        SCIENCE. New York: Holt, Rinehart and
        Winston, 1961.

Buchanan, Robert Angus. TECHNOLOGY AND SOCIAL
        PROGRESS. Oxford: Pergamon Press, 1965.

Etzioni, Amitai, ed. SOCIAL CHANGE: SOURCES,
        PATTERNS, AND CONSEQUENCES. New York:
        Basic Books, 1964.

Finkle, Jason L., ed. POLITICAL DEVELOPMENT AND
        SOCIAL CHANGE. New York: John Wiley,
        1966.

Hagan, Everett Einar. ON THE THEORY OF SOCIAL
        CHANGE: HOW ECONOMIC GROWTH BEGINS. A
        Study from the Center for International
        Studies, M.I.T., Homewood, Ill: Dorsey
        Press, 1962.

Hoffer, Eric. THE ORDEAL OF CHANGE. New York:
        Harper and Row, 1963.

Hogben, Herbert Ian. SOCIAL CHANGE. London:
        Watts, 1958.

Mead,   Margaret.   CONTINUITIES   IN   CULTURAL
          EVOLUTION. New Haven: Yale University
          Press, 1964.

          ed. CULTURAL PATTERNS AND TECHNICAL
          CHANGE. A Manual prepared for the World
          Federation for Mental Health, UNESCO,
          1953.

Moore, Wilbert Ellis, ed.   READINGS CN SOCIAL
CHANGE.

          SOCIAL CHANGE. Englewcod Cliffs, N.J.:
          Prentice Hall, 1965.

Neal, Marie Augusta.   VALUES AND INTERESTS IN
          SOCIAL CHANGE. Englewocd Cliffs, N.J.:
          Prentice Hall, 1965.

Odegard, Peter H. POLITICAL POWER AND SOCIAL
          CHANGE. New Brunswick, N.J.:   Rutgers
          University Press, 1966.

Ogburn, William Fielding. ON CULTURE AND SOCIAL
          CHANGE: SELECTED PAPERS.   Edited and
          with an introduction by Ctis Dudley
          Duncan, Chicago: University of Chicago
          Press, 1964.

Ruopp, Phillips, ed. APPROACHES TO COMMUNITY
          DEVELOPMENT: A Symposium Introductory to
          Problems and Methods of Village Welfare
          in   Underdevelcped   Areas.   With   a
          Foreword   by   S.   Radha-Krishnan, The
          Hague: W. van Hceve, 1953.

Spicer, Edward Holland, ed. HUMAN PROBLEMS IN
          TECHNOLOGICAL CHANGE. A Casebook.   New
          York: Russell Sage Foundaticn, 1952.

de Vries, Egbert.   MAN IN RAPID SCCIAL CHANGE.
          Garden City, N.Y.: Doubleday, 1961.

Zollschan, George K., ed. EXPLORATICNS IN SOCIAL
          CHANGE. Boston: Houghtcn Mifflin, 1964.

SOME   GENERAL   THEORETICAL   WORKS   CN AFRICAN
NATIONALISM:

Bartlett, Vernon. STRUGGLE FOR AFRICA. New York:
          F.A. Praeger, 1953.

Carter, Gwendolen M. INDEPENDENCE FOR AFRICA. New
          York: Praeger, 1960.

Hatch, John C. AFRICA TODAY AND TOMORROW: AN
OUTLINE OF BASIC FACTS AND MAJOR
PROBLEMS. New York: Praeger, 1960.

Hodgkin, Thomas Lionel. NATIONALISM IN COLONIAL
AFRICA. New York: New York University
Press, 1957.

Koh, Hans. AFRICAN NATIONALISM IN THE TWENTIETH
CENTURY. Princeton, N.J.: Van Nostrand,
1965.

Perham, Margery Freda. THE COLONIAL RECKONING:
THE END OF IMPERIAL RULE IN AFRICA IN
THE LIGHT OF BRITISH EXPERIENCE. New
York: Knopf, 1962.

Ritner, Peter. THE DEATH OF AFRICA. New York:
Macmillan, 1960.

Sampson, Anthony. COMMON SENSE ABOUT AFRICA. New
York: Macmillan, 1961.

Sithole, Ndabaningi. AFRICAN NATIONALISM. New
York: Oxford University Press, 1959.

Wauthier, Claude. THE LITERATURE AND THOUGHT OF
MODERN AFRICA. New York: F.A. Praeger,
1967.

III. Evolution Of Protest Movements

Apter, David E. "The Role of Traditionalism in
the Political Modernization of Ghana and
Uganda", WORLD POLITICS, XIII (1960),
pp. 45-68.

Austin, Dennis. POLITICS IN GHANA, 1946-1960
Oxford: Clarendon Press, 1964.

Berg, Elliot J. "The Economic Basis of Political
Choice in French West Africa", AMERICA
POLITICAL SCIENCE REVIEW, LIV (1960) pp
391-405.

Coleman, James S. "The Emergence of Africa
Political Parties", in C. Grove Haines
ed., AFRICA TODAY, (Baltimore: John
Hopkins Press, 1955), pp. 225-256.

"Nationalism in Tropical Africa"
AMERICAN POLITICAL SCIENCE REVIEW
XLVIII (1954), pp. 404-426.

Deutch,   Karl   W.   NATIONALISM   AND   SOCIAL
            COMMUNICATION: AN   INQUIRY   INTO   THE
            FOUNDATIONS   OF   NATIONALITY.   London:
            Chapman and Hall, 1953.

            "Social   Mobilization   and   Political
            Development", AMERICAN POLITICAL SCIENCE
            REVIEW, LV (1961), pp. 493-514.

Emerson, Rupert. FROM EMPIRE TO NATION: THE RISE
            TO SELF ASSERTION OF ASIA AND AFRICAN
            PEOPLES. Cambridge: Harvard University
            Press, 1960.

            "Nationalism and Political Development",
            JOURNAL OF POLITICS, XXII (1960), pp. 3-
            28.

Hodgkin, Thomas.   AFRICAN POLITICAL PARTIES: AN
            INTRODUCTORY   GUIDE.   Harmondsworth,
            Middlesex: Pengium Books, 1961.

            NATIONALISM IN COLONIAL AFRICA. London:
            Frederick Muller, 1956.

            "The New West Africa State System",
            UNIVERSITY OF TORONTO QUARTERLY, XXXI
            (1961), pp. 74-82.

            "A Note on the Language of African
            Nationalism", in Kenneth Kirkwood, ed.,
            AFRICAN   AFFAIRS,   NUMBER   ONE,   St.
            Anthony's Papers No. 10 (London: Chatto
            & Windus, 1961), pp. 22-40.

Hunter,   Guy. THE NEW SOCIETIES OF TROPICAL
            AFRICA: A SELECTIVE STUDY.   London:
            Oxford University Press for Institute of
            Race Relations, 1962.

O. Mannoni. PROSPERO AND CALIBAN: A STUDY OF THE
            PSYCHOLOGY   OF   COLONISATION   London:
            Metheun & Co., 1956.

Mazrui,   Ali   A.   "Consent, Colonialism, and
            Sovereignty", POLITICAL   STUDIES,   XI
            (1963), pp. 36-55.

            "On the Concept 'We are All Africans'"
            AMERICAN POLITICAL SCIENCE REVIEW, LVII
            (1963), pp. 88-97.

Schacter, Ruth. "Single-Party Systems in West
            Africa", AMERICAN   POLITICAL   SCIENCE
            REVIEW, LV (1961), pp. 294-307.

Wallerstein, Immanuel.   AFRICA: THE POLITICS OF
        INDEPENDENCE.   New York: Vintage Books,
        1961.

    IV.   Pan-Africanism And Regional Integration

American Society of African Culture, ed., PAN-
        AFRICANISM RECONSIDERED, Berkeley and
        Los Angeles: University of California
        Press, 1962.

Awooner-Renner.   WEST   AFRICAN   SOVIET   UNION.
        London: WANS Press, 1962.

Azikiwe, Nnamdi.   THE FUTURE OF PAN-AFRICANISM.
        London: Nigeria   High   Commissioner,
        1961.

Cox ,   Richard.   PAN-AFRICANISM IN PRACTICE:
        PAFMECSA 1958-1964.   London: Oxford
        University Press for Institute of Race
        Relations, 1964.

Cronon, Edmund D.   BLACK MOSES: THE STORY OF
        MARCUS GARVEY AND THE UNIVERSAL NEGRO
        IMPROVEMENT   ASSOCIATION.   Madison:
        University of Wisconsin Press, 1955.

DuBois, W.E. Burghardt.   THE WORLD AND AFRICA.
        New York: Viking Press, 1947.

Emerson, Rupert. "Pan-Africanism", INTERNATIONAL
        ORGANIZATION, XVI (1962), pp. 275-290.

Henry, Paul-Marc.   "Pan-Africanism: A Dream Come
        True", FOREIGN AFFAIRS, XXXVII (1959),
        pp. 443-452.

Legum, Colin. PAN-AFRICANISM: A SHORT POLITICAL
        GUIDE. London: Pall Mall, 1962.

Lessing, Pieter. "Problems of 'Pan-Africa'", THE
        LISTENER, Sept. 22, 1960. pp. 453-455.

McWilliams, Wilson C., and Jonathan Wise Polier.
        "Pan-Africanism and the Dilemmas   of
        National   Development",Phylon,   XXV
        (1964), pp. 44-64.

Nye, Joseph S., Jr.   PAN-AFRICANISM AND EAST
        AFRICAN   INTEGRATION.   Cambridge:
        Harvard University Press, 1965.

"Unification in Africa: Six Traps in
Search of a Scholar", in John D.
Montgomery and Arthur Smittnes, eds.,
PUBLIC POLICY, XIII (Cambridge: Harvard
University Press, 1964), pp. 358-368.

OConnell, Father J. "Senghor, Nkrumah and Azikiwe:
Unity and Diversity in West African
States", NIGERIAN JOURNAL OF ECONOMIC
AND SOCIAL STUDIES, V (1963), pp. 77-93.

Padmore, George, ed. HISTORY OF THE PAN-AFRICAN
CONFERENCE. London: Hammersmith
Eookshop, 1963 (reprint).

PAN-AFRICANISM CR COMMUNISM? THE COMING
STRUGGLE FOR AFRICA. Dennis Dobson,
1956.

Sanger, Clyde. "Toward Unity in Africa", FOREIGN
AFFAIRS, XLII (1964), pp. 269-281.

V. Politics Of Integration And African Unity.

Bascom, William R. "Tribalism, Nationalism and
Pan-Africanism", ANNALS OF THE AMERICAN
ACADEMY OF POLITICAL AND SOCIAL SCIENCE,
CCCXLII (1962), pp. 22-29.

Binder, Leonard. "National Integration and
Political Development", AMERICAN
POLITICAL SCIENCE REVIEW, LVIII (1964),
pp. 622-631.

Boutros-Ghali, Boutros. "The Addis Ababa
Charter", INTERNATIONAL CONCILIATION,
CXLVI (January, 1964).

Coleman, James S. "The Problem of Political
Integration in Emergent Africa", WESTERN
POLITICAL QUARTERLY, VIII (March 1955),
pp. 44-58.

Coleman, James S. and Carl G. Rosberg., eds.
POLITICAL AND NATIONAL INTEGRATION IN
TROPICAL AFRICA. Berkeley and Los
Angeles: University of California
Press, 1964.

Kilson, Martin L. "Authoritarian and Single-Party
Tendencies in African Politics", WORLD
POLITICS, XV (1963), pp. 262-294.

"African Political Change and the
Modernization Process", JOURNAL OF

MODERN AFRICAN STUDIES, I (1963), pp. 425-440.

Nkrumah, Kwame. "African Prospect", FOREIGN AFFAIRS. XXXVII (1958), pp. 45-53.

I SPEAK OF FREEDOM. London: Heineman, 1961.

AFRICA MUST UNITE. New York: Praeger, 1963.

Padelford, Norman J. "The Organization of African Unity", INTERNATIONAL ORGANIZATION, XVIII (1964), pp. 521-542.

Wallerstein, Immanuel. "Ethnicity and National Integration in West Africa", CAHIERS D'ETUDES AFRICAINES, III (October, 1960), pp. 129-138.

Zolberg, Aristide R. "Mass Parties and National Integration: The Case of the Ivory Coast", JOURNAL OF POLITICS, XXV (1963), pp. 36-48.

VI. Newspapers And Party Publications.

THE ASHANTI PIONEER   (Kumasi, Ghana)

THE DAILY ECHO   (Accra, Ghana)

THE DAILY EXPRESS   (Accra, Ghana)

THE DAILY GRAPHIC   (Accra, Ghana)

THE EVENING NEWS   (Accra, Ghana)

THE EWE NEWSLETTER   (Accra), Nos. 1-41.
                           May 1945-September
                           1948.

FREEDOM   C.P.P. Monthly
                           (Accra, Ghana)

THE GHANAIAN TIMES   (Accra, Ghana)

PAN-AFRICAN   C.P.P. Monthly
                               (Accra, Ghana)

THE PARTY   C.P.P. Bi-Weekly
                           (Accra, Ghana)

THE DAWN   C.P.P. Bi-Weekly

(London)

VII. Bibliography For Dissertation

Acquah, Abednego G. THE FANTSE OF GHANA. (Hull,
       England undated).

Allot, A. ESSAYS IN AFRICAN LAW (London, 1960).

Almond, Gabriel A. "A Developmental Approach to
       Political Systems", WORLD POLITICS
       (January, 1965), pp. 180-190.

Apter, David E. "Nkrumah, Charisma, and the
       Coup", DAEDALUS (Summer 1968), pp. 757-
       792.

       GHANA IN TRANSITION. New York, 1963.

Arden-Clarke, Charles. "Eight Years in the Gold
       Coast", AFRICAN AFFAIRS, (January,
       1958).

Aron, Raymond. "Social Structure and Ruling
       Class", BRITISH JOURNAL OF SOCIOLOGY
       (1950).

Ashby, Eric. AFRICAN UNIVERSITIES AND WESTERN
       TRADITION. Cambridge, 1964.

AXIOMS OF KWAME NKRUMAH. Freedom Fighters'
       Edition, London, Panaf Publications
       Ltd., 1967.

Berger, Monroe, et. al., eds. "The Problem of
       Authority", FREEDOM AND CONTROL IN
       MODERN SOCIETY. New York, 1954.

Blake, J.W. EUROPEAN BEGINNINGS IN WEST AFRICA,
       1454-1578, (London, 1937).

       EUROPEANS IN WEST AFRICA, 1450-1650,
       Vol. I & II. (London, Hatluyt Society,
       1942).

Busia, K.A. THE POSITION OF THE CHIEF IN THE
       MODERN POLITICAL SYSTEM OF ASHANTI
       (London, 1958).

Cantril, H. THE PSYCHOLOGY OF SOCIAL MOVEMENTS.
       New York, 1941.

Committee on Constitutional Reform, 1949.
       Colonial No. 248 (Coussey Commission).

Cowan, Gray L. et. al. eds., EDUCATION AND NATION-EUILDING IN AFRICA. New York, 1965.

Debray, Regis. REVCLUTICN IN THE REVCIUTICN. New York, Grove Press, 1967.

DeVries, Egbert. MAN IN RAPIL SCCIAL CHANGE. Garden City, New York, 1961.

Duverger, Maurice. POLITICAL PARTIES (New York, 1957).

Editors of The Spark, SCME ESSENTIAL FEATURES OF NKRUMAISM. New York. International Publishers, 1965.

Eisenstadt, S.N. MODEFNIZATICN: PROTEST AND CHANGE. Englewood Cliffs, N.J., 1966).

Fage, F.D. AN INTRODUCTICN TO THE HISTORY OF WEST AFRICA (Cambridge: England, 1961).

Fanon, Frantz. THE WRETCHED OF THE EARTH. New York, 1964.

GHANA YOUTH MANIFESTO. Accra, Ghana, 1948.

GHANA: Seven-Year Develcpment Plan, 1963/64 to 1969/70. Accra, Ghana.

Hagen, Everet E. ON THE THEORY OF SOCIAL CHANGE. Hcmewood, Ill., The Dorsey Press, 1962.

Harbiscn, Frederick. "The Prime Movers of Innovation", ELUCATICN AND ECONOMIC LEVELOPMENT. C. Arnold, et. al. eds., Chicago, 1965.

Jchnstcn, Sir Harry. The Histcry of the Colcnization of Africa by Alien Races (Cambridge, England, 1913).

Kilscn, Martin, "African Autccracy", AFRICA TODAY (April, 1966).

Kimble, David. A POLITICAL HISTCRY OF GHANA 1850-1928. Oxford, 1963.

Kohn, H. "Pan-Movements", ENCYCLCFEDIA OF THE SOCIAL SCIENCES. New York, 1933, XI.

Levy, M. THE STRUCTURE OF SOCIETY. Princeton, Princeton University Press, 1952.

Loewenstein, Karl. MAX WEBER's POLITICAL IDEAS IN
THE PERSPECTIVE OF OUR TIME. Amherst,
1966.

Lucas, Sir Charles. THE PARTITION AND
COLONIZATION OF AFRICA. (Oxford, 1922).

Marx, Karl. KRITIK DES HEGELSCHEN STAATRECHTS,
translated in KARL MARX: SELECTED
WRITINGS. ed. by T.B. Bottomore. New
York, 1964.

Mills, C.W. SOCIOLOGICAL IMAGINATION, New York,
1959.

Nkrumah, Kwame. GHANA — THE AUTOBIOGRAPHY OF
KWAME NKRUMAH. (London, 1965).

Speech by Kwame Nkrumah to the National Assembly
of Ghana on October 2, 1962.

Nkrumah, Kwame. GUIDE TO PARTY ACTION. Accra,
Ghana. February 3, 1962.

Speech by Kwame Nkrumah at the laying of the
Foundation Stone of the Institute at
Winneba on February 18, 1961.

Nkrumah, Kwame. BLUEPRINT FOR THE FUTURE.
Accra, Ghana. August 24, 1965.

"African Socialism Revisited", AFRICAN
FORUM, Vol. I, No. 3, Winter 1966, pp.
4-12.

Speech to the Indian Council on World
Affairs, New Delhi, December 26, 1958.

Address to the National Assembly of
Ghana. June 12, 1965.

"Dawn Broadcast", Accra, Ghana, (April
8, 1961).

Speech at the Opening of the Institute
of African Studies. Legon, Ghana,
October 25, 1963.

Speech at the Opening Ceremony of Akuafo
Hall of Residence at the University
College of the Gold Coast, February 17,
1956.

Speech delivered at a University Dinner, University of Ghana, Legon, Ghana, on February 24, 1963.

Speech at the Seminar for Senior Civil Servants at Winneba, Ghana, April 14, 1962.

Speech at the laying of the Foundation Stone of the Atomic Reactor at Kwabenya, Ghana, November 25, 1964.

Nyerere, Julius. "The Future of African Nationalism", TRIBUNE (London, May 27, 1960).

Padmore, George. GOLD COAST REVOLUTION (London, 1953).

Padover, Saul K. THOMAS JEFFERSON ON DEMOCRACY. New York, 1961.

Parsons, Talcott "Some Considerations on the Theory of Social Change", RURAL SOCIOLOGY, 26, September 1961. pp. 220-234.

Phelps-Stokes Fund, EDUCATION IN AFRICA: A STUDY OF WEST AND EQUATORIAL AFRICA. New York, 1922.

"Preamble Proposals for a Federal Constitution for an Independent Gold Coast and Togoland by Movements and Parties other than the Convention People's Party". Kumasi, Ghana, u.d.

Pratt, S. and Loveridge, A.J. "Training Programs Manpower Planning", TEACHER EDUCATION, IV, 3 (London, February 1964). pp. 179-190.

PROGRAMME OF THE CONVENTION PEOPLE'S PARTY FOR WORK AND HAPPINESS. Accra, Ghana, 1961.

Prospectus of the Kwame Nkrumah Ideological Institute, Winneba, Ghana, i.d.

REPORT OF THE COMMISSION ON UNIVERSITY EDUCATION. December 1960 - January 1961.

Report of the Watson Commission. Accra, Ghana, 1948.

Rivlin, Benjamin. "The Concept of Political System in the Study of Developing States", Orbis, X, 2 (Summer, 1966) pp. 548-563.

Robinson, K. and Mackenzie, W.J. FIVE AFRICAN ELECTIONS. Oxford, 1960.

Saloway, R. "The New Gold Coast", INTERNATIONAL AFFAIRS, October 1955.

Seligman, G. LEADERSHIP IN A NEW NATION: POLITICAL DEVELOPMENT IN ISRAEL. New York, 1964.

"Political Recruitment and Party Structure", and "The Study of Political Leadership", THE AMERICAN POLITICAL SCIENCE REVIEW, XLIV (1950) pp. 904-915.

Senghor, L. AFRICAN SOCIALISM., cited in C.F. Andrian, "Democracy and Socialism", in David E. Apter, ed., IDEOLOGY AND DISCONTENT. Glencoe, 1964.

Shils, Edward. "The Theory of Mass Movements", DIOGENES. XXXIX (1963), pp. 45-66.

Sithole, Ndabaningi. AFRICAN NATIONALISM. Cape Town, 1959.

Smith, Edwin W. AGGREY OF AFRICA. (New York, 1929).

Sorokin, Pitrim A. THE SOCIOLOGY OF REVOLUTION. Philadelphia, J.B. Lippincott, 1925.

Statement by the Government on the Report of the Commission on University Education. WHITE PAPER No. 5161, Accra, Ghana.

UNIVERSITY OF GHANA REPORT. October 26, 1962.

UNO "International Survey of Programs of Social Development", New York, 1959.

Weber, Max. THEORY OF SOCIAL AND ECONOMIC ORGANIZATION, New York, 1947.

ESSAYS IN SOCIOLOGY. Translated by H.H. Gerth and C.W. Mills, New York, 1946.

Wilson, John. EDUCATION AND CHANGING WEST AFRICAN CULTURE. New York, 1963.

Wriggins, Howard. "Aggregaticn cf Power-An Approach to Politics in Emerging Countries". INTERNATICNAL STUDIES ASSOCIATICN PROCEEDINGS. (April, 1965).

Wright, Richard. BLACK POWER-A RECORD OF REACTIONS IN A LAND CF PATHOS. New York, 1954.

Youth Ccnference Pamphlet. FIRST STEPS TOWARDS A NATICNAL FUND Achimota, Ghana, 1938.

Agriculture
  Self-Employed
   Farmers   1,300,000   1,337,500   37,500
  Other Farm
   Employment   200,000   250,000   50,000
                     ──────────   ──────────   ──────
   Sub-Total   1,500,000   1,587,500   87,500
   Per cent   60%   54%

   GRAND TOTAL   2,504,000   2,997,000   493,000
        MALE   1,504,000
      FEMALE   1,000,000
──

28	200,000	237,500	18 %
25	12,500	62,500	31 %
5	212,500	300,000	20 %
19	600,000	1,093,000	43 %

APPENDIX

(The source of the tables that follow is: GHANA: SEVEN-YEAR DE

TABLE I

GHANA MANPOWER PROJECTIONS 1963-1970.

	Employment 1963	Required by 1970	in Employment 1970	for Wa over 1963	
High-Level					
Administrative-					
Managerial	13,000		16,000	3,000	
Professional	19,000		24,000	5,000	
Sub-Professionals					
and Technical	7,000		19,000	12,000	
Skilled Crafts	36,000		52,000	16,000	
Primary/Middle					
Teachers	32,000		69,000	37,000	
Secondary and					
Higher Teachers	2,000		6,000	4,000	
Sub Total	109,000		186,000	77,000	
Per cent	4%		7%		
Middle-Level					
Clerical and					
Commercial	43,000		65,000	22,000	
Trade (Excl. of					
Petty Traders)	46,000		69,000	23,000	
Mining	33,000		42,000	9,000	
Transportation/					
Communication	63,000		105,500	42,500	
Semi-Skilled					
Craft &					
Operatives	156,000		237,000	81,000	
Services	54,000		80,000	26,000	
Sub-Total	395,000		598,500	203,000	
Per cent	16%		19%		
Unskilled					
Petty Traders	300,000		330,000	30,000	
Tailors etc.	75,000		82,500	7,000	
Bakers etc.	45,000		68,000	23,000	
Laborers	80,000		144,500	64,000	
Sub-Total	500,000		625,000	125,000	
Per cent	20%		20%		

stage by 1970	Needed by 1970	to Employment 1963	
23	3,900	6,900	53 %
26	5,700	10,700	56 %
171	2,000	14,000	200 %
44	10,800	26,800	74 %
115	9,000	46,000	143 %
200	600	4,600	230 %
70	32,000	109,000	100 %
51	15,900	37,900	88 %
50	16,000	39,000	84 %
27	15,000	24,000	72 %
67	25,300	67,800	107 %
51	58,800	139,800	89 %
48	24,500	50,000	93 %
51	155,500	359,000	90 %
10	100,000	130,000	43 %
10	26,000	33,500	44 %
51	30,000	53,000	117 %
80	44,000	108,500	135 %
25	200,000	325,000	65 %

FRANCIS A. BOTCHWAY
                       TABLE III

PROJECTED ENROLMENT IN PRIMARY, MIDDLE, AND
       CONTINUING SCHOOLS AND TEACHER
             REQUIREMENTS, 1964-1970

Year	School Population at end of Last Year	New Number of Pass-Outs	Teachers Pupils Net Enrolled	Additional Total Alrea Enrolment at
1964	1,303,000	49,000	244,000*	1,498,000
1965	1,498,000	60,000	240,000*	1,6
1966	1,678,000	64,000	236,000	1,85
1967	1,850,000	65,000	244,000	2,0
1968	2,028,500	125,000	253,000	2,1
1969	2,156,500	220,000	262,000	2,1
1970	2,198,500	250,000	271,000	2,2
	---	833,500	---	13,6

Note (1)   *Enrolments in 1964 and 1965 exceed the ce
            the age of six. This increase is to brin
            do not join the school system at age 6.
            figures are normal.

     (2)   These projections do not take into accoun
            dropouts.

	dy Post	Teachers Required	
37,250		4,875	
78,000	42,125	4,500	
0,000	46,625	4,300	
28,500	50,925	4,460	
56,500	55,385	3,200	
98,500	58,585	1,050	
19,500	59,635	525	
29,000	---	22,910	

nsus figures of children reaching
g in children aged 7, 8 and 9 who
Thereafter the enrolment

t any wastage resulting from

178

FRANCIS A. BOTCHWAY
TABLE V

PROJECTED ENROLMENT IN SECONDARY SCHOOLS AND
TEACHER REQUIREMENTS (1964-70)

Year	Old Pupils	Passing Out	Net Number of Pupils	Total of New Pupils	Additional Total Enrolment	Teachers Required
1964	28,500	3,500	25,000	10,000	35,0	
1965	25,000	4,000	31,000	12,000	45,0	
1966	43,000	4,500	38,500	14,000	52,5	
1967	52,500	14,500	38,000	16,000	54,0	
1968	54,000	10,000	44,000	18,000	62,0	
1969	62,000	12,000	50,000	20,000	70,0	
1970	70,000	14,000	56,000	22,000	78,0	
	---	62,500	---	112,000	--	

Teachers
    Required

00	1,575	325
00	1,975	400
00	2,450	475
00	3,000	550
00	3,400	400
00	3,900	500
00	4,300	400
–	4,300	3,050

TABLE VI

TEACHER TRAINING COLLEGES: ENROLMENT AND TEACHERS
(1964-70)

Year	Number Old Students	Number Students Out	Enrolment	Number of Additional Passing Staff	College Required	Staff
1964	6,000	5,000	11,000	2,000	755	200
1965	9,000	5,000	14,000	2,000	955	200
1966	12,000	6,000	18,000	5,000	1,155	200
1967	13,000	6,000	19,000	5,000	1,225	66
1968	14,000	6,000	20,000	5,000	1,291	66
1969	15,000	6,000	21,000	6,000	1,357	66
1970	15,000	6,000	21,000	6,000	1,357	0
		40,000		31,000	8,095	798

FRANCIS A. BOTCHWAY

TABLE VII

OUTPUT FROM APPRENTICE TRAINING AND
TECHNICAL EDUCATION
1964-70

	Products from Apprentice Training		Products from Technical Training Institutes		
Year	Craftsmen	Advanced Craft Training (Senior Technicians)	Junior Technicians	Total Columns 3-4

Year				
1964	205	90	835	925
1965	300	150	835	985
1966	500	150	835	985
1967	700	300	1,200	1,500
1968	900	500	1,275	1,775
1969	1,000	500	1,350	1,850
1970	1,000	500	1,425	1,925
TOTAL	4,605	2,190	7,755	9,945

TABLE VIII

CLERICAL-COMMERCIAL EDUCATION
(1964-70)

CLERICAL CERTIFICATE TRAINING (POST-PRIMARY)

Year	New Students	Cutflow	Teachers Required (1:20)
1964	1,500	---	75
1965	1,500	1,500	75
1966	1,500	1,500	75
1967	1,500	1,500	75
1968	1,500	1,500	75
1969	1,500	1,500	75
1970	1,500	1,500	75
		9,000	75

COMMERCIAL DIPLOMA (POST-SECONDARY)

Year	New Students	Outflow	Teachers Required (1:20)
1964	500	---	25
1965	500	500	25
1966	500	500	25
1967	500	500	25
1968	500	500	25
1969	500	500	25
1970	500	500	25
		3,000	25